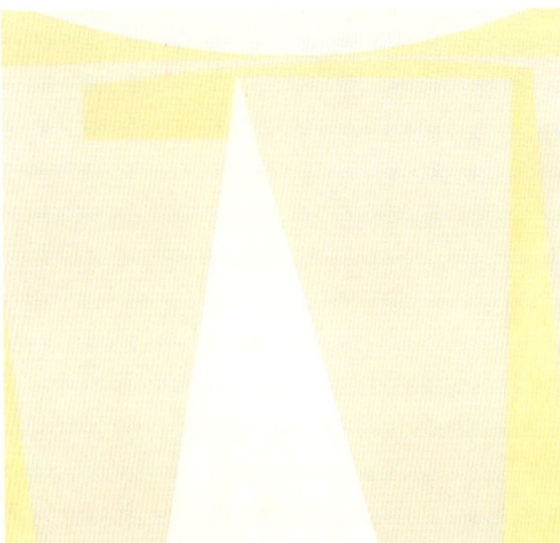

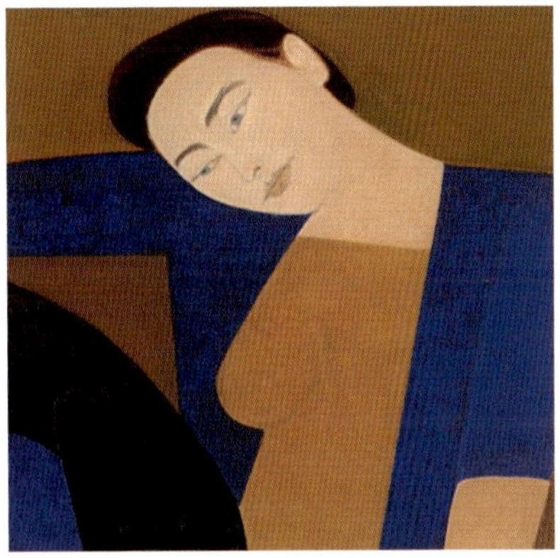

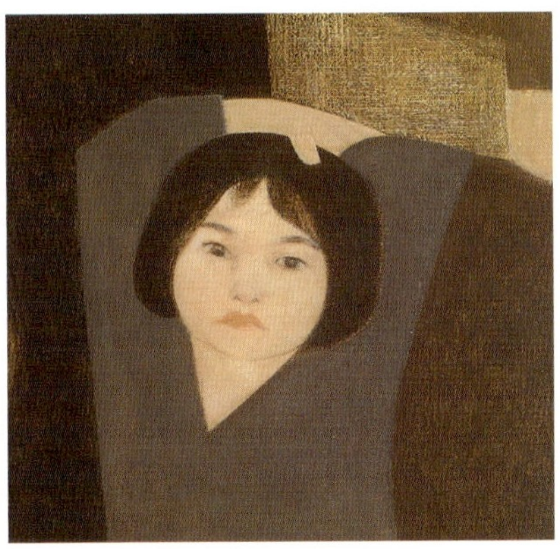

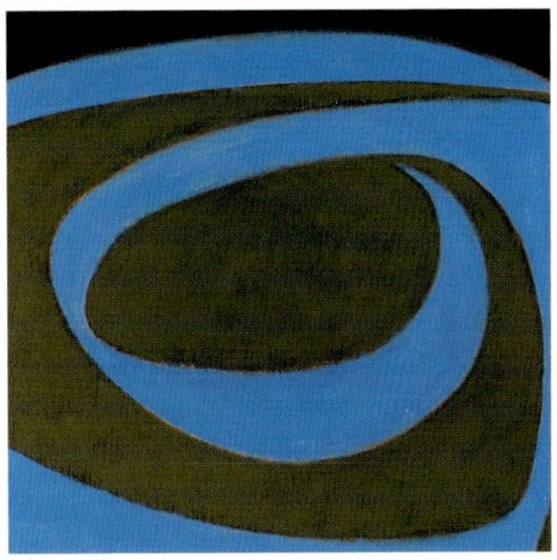

WILL BARNET

Palmer Museum of Art
The Pennsylvania State University
University Park, Pennsylvania

Painting without Illusion

The Genesis of Four Works from the 1960s

Patrick J. McGrady
Charles V. Hallman Curator

Palmer Museum of Art
May 10 – October 5, 2003

Alexandre Gallery
October 16 – November 29, 2003

Front cover: Will Barnet, *Mother and Child*, detail, 1961
Oil on canvas, 46 x 39 inches
Collection of the artist
Courtesy Alexandre Gallery, New York

Back cover: Will Barnet, *Enclosure*, detail, 1962/2003
Oil on canvas, 46 x 39 inches
Courtesy Alexandre Gallery, New York

Page 1, 32: clockwise, from upper left:

Will Barnet, *Eden*, detail, 1964–65
Oil on canvas, 88 x 43 inches
Courtesy Alexandre Gallery, New York

Will Barnet, *The Blue Robe*, detail, 1962
Oil on canvas, 50 x 54 inches
Collection of the artist
Courtesy Alexandre Gallery, New York

Will Barnet, *Enclosure*, detail, 1962/2003
Oil on canvas, 46 x 39 inches
Courtesy Alexandre Gallery, New York

Will Barnet, *Mother and Child*, detail, 1961
Oil on canvas, 46 x 39 inches
Collection of the artist
Courtesy Alexandre Gallery, New York

ISBN 0-911209-59-X

U. Ed. ARC 03-501
Library of Congress Control Number: 2003107857

Designed by Christie H. Zangrilli
Printed by Commercial Printing, State College, PA
Distributed by Penn State Press

PENNSTATE

College of Arts and Architecture

Contents

Foreword

Jan Keene Muhlert, *Director*

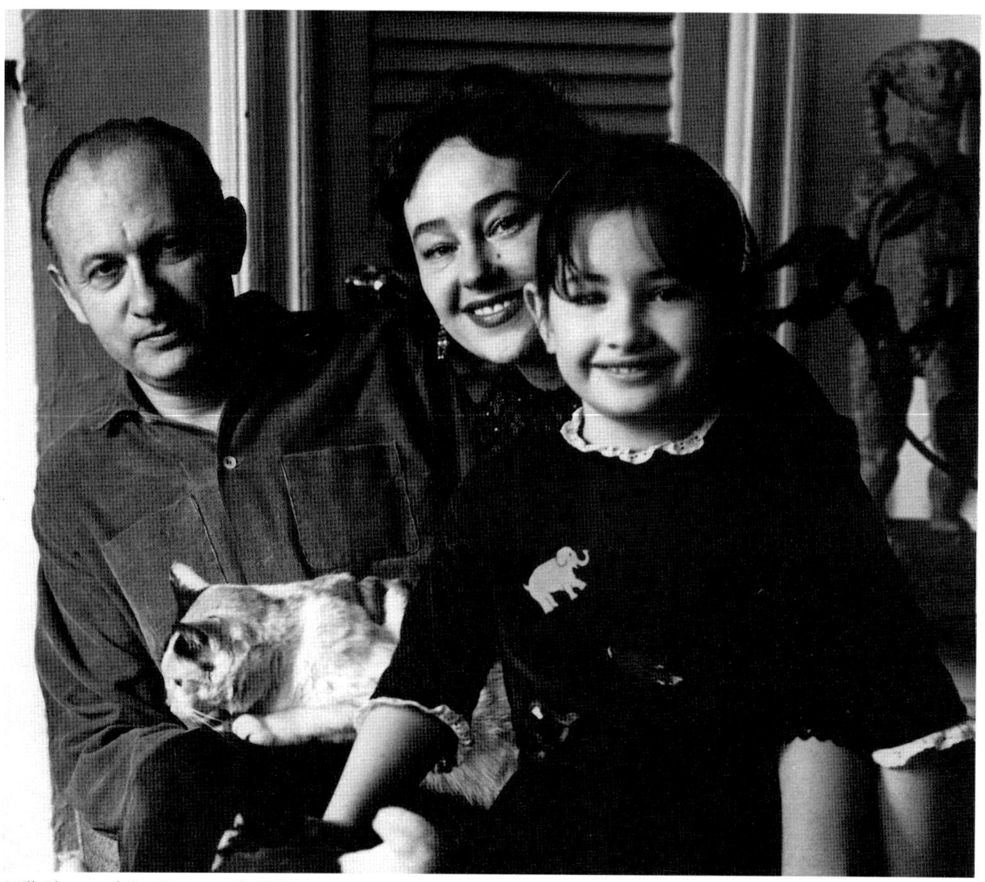

Will, Elena, and Ona Barnet, early 1960s.

In the summer of 1965, and then again the following spring, Will Barnet was invited to Penn State by Wirth McCoy, then head of the Department of Art, to offer courses in painting and printmaking. McCoy was well aware of Will's teaching credentials, having been instrumental in securing his residency two years earlier at Washington State University, and so he bestowed upon the artist the title of *Distinguished* Visiting Professor. Will's tenure at Penn State began on the heels of a successful exhibition of his Spokane paintings at Grippi & Waddell Gallery in New York, and during both visits, after fulfilling his daily teaching responsibilities, he worked on the plates for prints based on the Spokane series. In fact, trial proofs for the aquatint *Compression–Spokane* were pulled, with the assistance of faculty member (and now professor emeritus) Bruce Shobaken, in the spring of 1966.[1]

The residency succeeded splendidly, producing results common to all such visits Will has made throughout his career. "The young MFA candidate who assisted Will," McCoy later wrote, "confided to me that he had learned more about excellence and art during his brief five weeks with Will than he'd learned during his entire previous schooling. He said that the association with Will had raised the quality of his own vision to a level he had previously not considered possible!"[2]

McCoy greatly admired Will's work, and was especially taken with the canvases he viewed during a visit to the artist's New York studio early in 1965. "They are extremely beautiful," he wrote of the most recent abstract paintings upon his return to State College, "and the large horizontal black one, the large square black one and the new one stand out in my mind as particularly important." He was equally attracted to the figural paintings Will had produced just a few years earlier, in a style to which he was just then returning. "All of the figurative things are lovely . . . ," he added in the same letter, "and, of course, I always loved the great beautiful one of Elena and Ona."[3] Together they planned an exhibition of some of these paintings to run concurrent with Will's residency; however, the exhibition failed to materialize, due mostly to commitments that sent the desired works elsewhere for the period they had in mind.

With *Will Barnet: Painting without Illusion*, we are delighted to have the opportunity, nearly forty years later, to place on view some of the pieces Wirth McCoy sought for that earlier exhibition. The "new one" of the three that struck him "as particularly important," is in all likelihood *Eden*, which Will completed during the winter of 1964–65, and the painting of Elena and Ona, Will's wife and daughter, is none other than *Mother and Child*. Both figure prominently in our exhibition.

This exhibition could not have succeeded without the assistance of Will Barnet. Over the past two years Will has generously found room in his still very active schedule to regularly meet with, and field countless phone calls from, the exhibition's curator, Patrick McGrady. In particular, we appreciate his enthusiastic and unwavering support as the project was narrowed to focus on just four of his paintings from the 1960s. We are likewise indebted to Elena Barnet, Will's devoted partner of fifty years.

We would like to thank Dr. and Mrs. Lawrence Dubin, Mrs. Barbara Fleischman, and another private collector for generously lending their works for this exhibition. A special word of gratitude goes to Terry Davis, for her financial support of the catalogue, and her earlier gifts of prints and watercolors by Will, which helped to initiate this project.

Phil Alexandre of Alexandre Gallery, and two members of his staff, Marie Evans, director, and Marit Knollmueller, associate director, have been enormously helpful in the organization of the exhibition, especially in their willingness to travel downtown to Will's studio at a moment's notice to find or photograph yet one more drawing. A word of thanks also goes to John Driscoll, director of Babcock Galleries, whose long-held appreciation of Will's work encouraged the development of this exhibition. We are most grateful to Patrick McGrady, Charles V. Hallman Curator, for planning the exhibition and overseeing the preparation of this catalogue. His essay adds a new perspective to the critical literature available on Will Barnet. The Palmer Museum of Art staff contributed significantly to the exhibition and catalogue alike, and Beverly Sutley, Ron Hand, Rich Hall, Betsy Warner, and Barbara Weaver deserve particular recognition for their efforts. Several persons from other institutions were responsible for providing images and resource material: Peter Spooner, curator, Tweed Museum of Art, University of Minnesota Duluth; Eileen Sullivan, assistant museum librarian, Photograph and Slide Library, The Metropolitan Museum of Art; and Michèle M. Wong, gallery manager and registrar, Grey Art Gallery, New York University.

Finally, we would like to recognize the following for their various contributions to this project: Richard Ackley, photographer, Campus Photography, School of Visual Arts, Penn State; G. Donald Bain, director, Geography Computing Facility, University of California Berkeley; Martha Fleischman, president, and Lillian Brenwasser, vice president, Kennedy Galleries; Carolyn Lucarelli, assistant curator, Department of Art History Slide Library, Penn State; Sarah Rich, assistant professor, Department of Art History, Penn State; Dorothy McCoy; and Bruce Shobaken, professor emeritus, School of Visual Arts, Penn State.

WILL BARNET

Painting without Illusion

The Genesis of Four Works from the 1960s

Patrick J. McGrady, *Charles V. Hallman Curator*

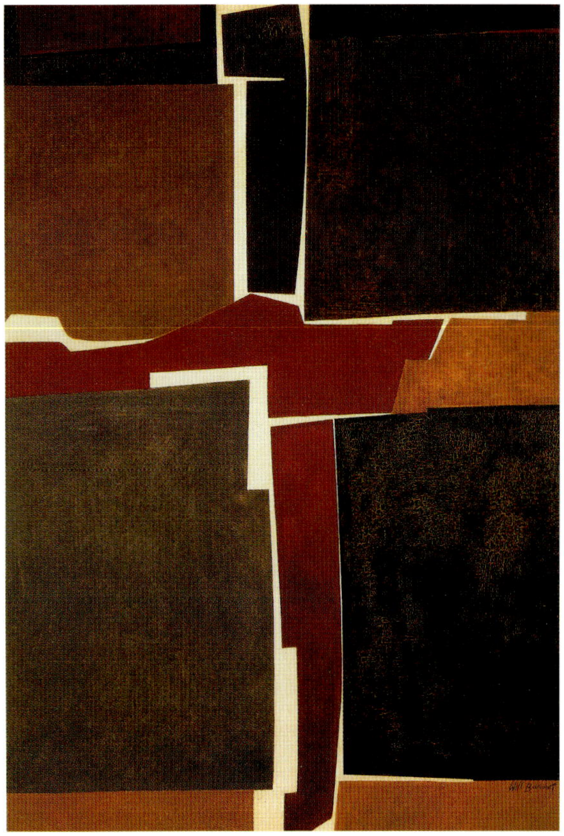

Fig. 1. Will Barnet, *Singular Image*, 1959. Oil on canvas, 68 1/2 x 46 inches. Private collection.

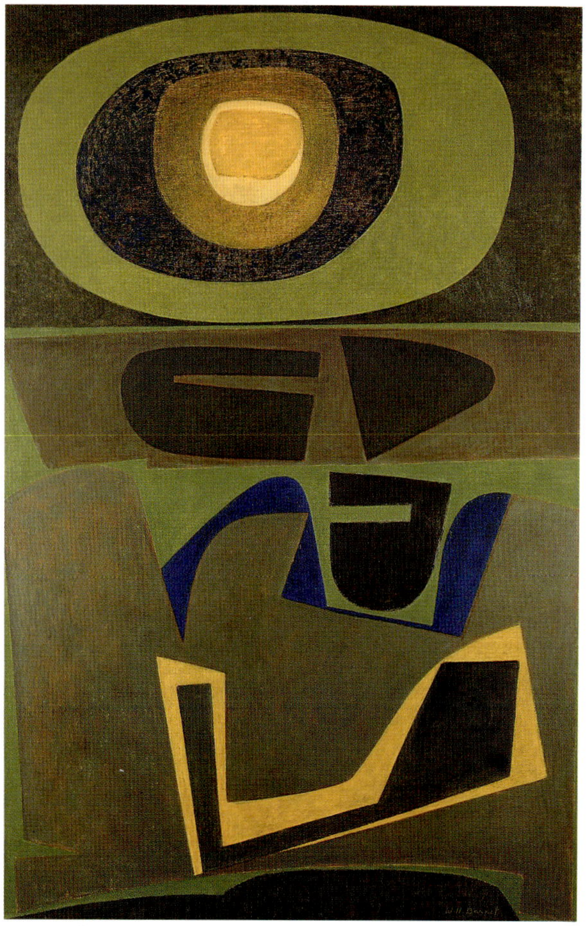

Fig. 2. Will Barnet, *Big Duluth*, 1960. Oil on canvas, 85 1/2 x 52 1/2 inches. Collection of the Tweed Museum of Art, University of Minnesota Duluth, Patrons and Subscribers Purchase Fund.

In February of 1960, Will Barnet celebrated nearly fifteen years of abstraction in his work with an exhibition at Bertha Schaefer Gallery in New York. The twelve paintings on view represented the most recent manifestations of a highly deliberated approach that had characterized the artist's efforts throughout his abstract period. In response, critics clearly recognized that with these canvases Barnet had reached an unprecedented moment in his career. "There is a silent grandeur," noted Dorothy Adlow in the *Christian Science Monitor*, "a hidden magic in these depictions in which color modulations are realized with exceptional sensitiveness."[1] Lawrence Campbell, reviewing for *Art News*, found the new works to be the finest of his career,[2] and Bennet Schiff of the *New York Post* concurred, writing:

> This is Barnet's best show, and another example of that always thrilling efflorescence which sometimes occurs in the life of a mature artist at a certain, magical time, when everything he's learned up to a point becomes clearly cohesive and touched with the true poetry of inspiration . . . . It seems clear to me that, with this show, Barnet is unquestionably in the forefront of today's American painters.[3]

Perhaps the most exemplary of this group is *Singular Image* (fig. 1). Although rooted, like all of Barnet's work, in an encounter with nature—in this instance, a glimpse of the artist's shadow as it intersected some cracks in a sidewalk[4]—countless studies and sketches have transformed objective references into a fully abstract design that plays itself out solely within the two-dimensional framework of the canvas. The shadowy figure has become a series of forms, confined within two narrow axes, which advance, or attempt to advance, against the four weighty quadrangles anchored in each corner. A strong upward thrust provides the principal movement, improbably enabled by the thin, clear line cutting between the vertical form in the lower center and the large plane to its right. These two elements want to collide, but they remain suspended almost infinitesimally apart, as if by some unseen force field. Like tectonic plates in motion, the energy transfers northward, toward the center, driving one of the segments along the horizontal axis into the planar block occupying the upper left quadrant. The offending form teeters, aiding movement further up the central axis with one shift, and with the opposite releasing tension across to the left edge.

At the top of the painting, and again at its base, linear shoots, formed by edges of contiguous planes and running perpendicular to the vertical axis, offer what are for the moment minor echoes of the main horizontal counterpoint. The thin wedges accompanying these gestures, however, threaten to amplify the incipient schisms, possibly to the point of rivaling the center and, at the same time, usurping much of the vertical column's dominance. These last details represent one of the more subtle, but also one of the more brilliant aspects of *Singular Image*. By bestowing a sense of *potential* kinesis, Barnet has imbued the painting with a life that lingers well beyond an initial reading. Such an effort is the mark of an artist at the height of his abstract powers, and is no doubt one of the pertinent reasons behind the adulatory reviews this and the other works in the group received upon their first showing.

Throughout his abstract period, Barnet derived most of his compositions from the human figure. For the longest time, landscape had bewildered him. "I never felt quite ready to cope with such an enormous element as this big space," he has admitted, "this tremendous scene, these millions of miles of space and planets that one sometimes can't even see or touch."[5] In the late 1950s, though, the confidence garnered from the success of his latest figure-inspired studies encouraged him to address as well the vistas experienced during his travels. After spending the summers of 1958 and 1959 in residence at the University of Minnesota in Duluth, he initiated a series of studies based on the captivating views near his accommodations on the shore of Lake Superior. The resulting canvases, completed in his New York studio in 1960, synthesized his emotional reactions to the region's vast expanse and the various celestial bodies reflecting across the surface of the lake.[6] In the most monumental of these paintings, *Big Duluth* (fig. 2), the arrangement of the abstracted forms facilitates a movement quite distinct from that found in *Singular Image*. The concentric bands enveloping the yellow disc in the uppermost section of the painting radiate elliptically to the left and right. The extrusive nature of the central color, however, particularly in juxtaposition with the increasingly complacent tones surrounding it, adds another dimension to the horizontal movement: outward, toward the viewer. Slightly fuller below, the emanating rings tug downward as well, approaching a brown banner that gently rises to greet the motion. The wedge-pierced form within this subjacent field echoes the curves of the encircling bands above, initiating a more powerful descent that cuts diagonally through inverted triangles of green and then sharper blue to the leg of the form furthest below. Glowing in chromatic harmony with the disc that heads the painting, this last image disperses the energy with an acute linear deflection to the right and, like its counterpart, out away from the picture plane as well.

Big Duluth and *Singular Image* were included, together with a number of similar canvases, in a major retrospective of Barnet's work during the summer of 1961 at the Institute of Contemporary Art in Boston. Although the paintings dated as early as 1940, nearly half had been completed within the past five years, making the exhibition a showcase for the artist's most recent abstractions. The newest painting, however, completed just a few months prior to the opening, was far more figural than anything Barnet had produced since the late 1940s. Still retaining a fair likeness of his wife and daughter, *Elena and Ona*, now know as *Mother and Child* (cat. no. 1), must have stood out as an anomaly against the dozens of abstract works that chronologically preceded it. Nonetheless, it passed without comment in the exhibition catalogue essay by Thomas Messer,[7] and received pleasant but undiscerning notice in local reviews of the show.[8]

Quite another reception awaited *Mother and Child* when it returned to New York and (still under the title *Elena and Ona*) joined several additional figural compositions in an early 1962 exhibition at Bertha Schaefer Gallery.[9] In anticipation of the scrutiny this new direction was sure to provoke, Barnet issued an explanatory statement for inclusion in the exhibition's press release:

> The same considerations which impelled me to work abstractly for the past ten years are present, though with a shift of focal reference, in this new group of paintings. There is no ambivalence for me in the fact that the figure has been profoundly transformed, or transposed, with closer reference to its original structure. Nor are there any so-called "humanistic" revelations for the present shift in my work.
>
> My interest has been in developing further the plastic convictions which have been evolving in my abstract work; so that a portrait, while remaining a portrait, should become in this sense an abstraction: the idea of a person in its most intense and essential aspect.[10]

The argument, or the works themselves, failed to convince, for although the exhibition received a few complimentary reviews, a number of critics, looking upon this new venture as almost *retardataire* in light of his abstract accomplishments, levied some of the most negative comments of Barnet's career. Labeling the newest paintings representational and thus comparable to the artist's offerings in the late 1940s, Natalie Edgar in *Art News* complained, "[t]he existence of intervening abstract years is undetectable in this show," and then wondered, "a case of artistic amnesia?" She accused him of reverting to outmoded ideas, calling the paintings "unavoidably academic," before politely concluding, "but within that class they are masterpieces."[11] More adverse was Brian O'Doherty's response in *The New York Times*:

> Will Barnet . . . is known as an abstractionist of the purist kind whose shapes are so thoroughly educated that they take their positions within the canvas like well-bred poodles. His sensibility in this genre is beyond reproach. Lately, however, the human figure has entered this abstract paradise, with results that leave his work sitting uneasily on the fence between abstraction and representation. It is an essentially false position.[12]

More important than the opinions of professional writers, however, was the reaction on the part of friends and close associates, many of whom wondered as well whether the artist had begun to veer from an inviolable path. Throughout much of the 1950s, Barnet had been a fervent member of the Association of Abstract Artists, created in 1936 to support a fledgling non-figurative movement in this country. AAA tended to lean toward a wholly structured approach to abstraction, particularly during the ascendancy of Abstract Expressionism, and this appealed to Barnet. He joined in 1954 and soon took on an active role within the group. In 1956, he co-edited *The World of Abstract Art*, a collection of essays issued to mark the organization's twentieth anniversary.[13] He also authored one of the volume's more cogent texts, in which he argued strongly in favor of the kind of architectonic non-objectivity that was beginning to distill in his painting.[14] So when, after years of heralding the AAA cause, Barnet turned so markedly to the figure—particularly in the wake of producing such successful canvases under its banner—he appeared to some to be abandoning abstraction wholeheartedly.

In fact, Barnet hadn't shifted all that much, for despite the introduction of perceptibly referential imagery, these new works remain highly abstract in composition. In *Mother and Child*, for example, nearly all of the painting's energy initiates near the upper right, with the mother's left arm. Moving across, the horizontal force lifts slightly at the shoulder, dislodging the head as the weight transfers, where cheek meets hand, diagonally through the right forearm. In tandem with a head now tilted slightly off axis, a wisp of displaced hair, a compactly arched brow, and an eye slightly askew all conspire to pivot the energy vertically as well, down the right drape of the mother's blackish brown robe and pooling in and around her lap. Complicit in this movement is the sweeping line that forms along the outer edge of the left arm above, and

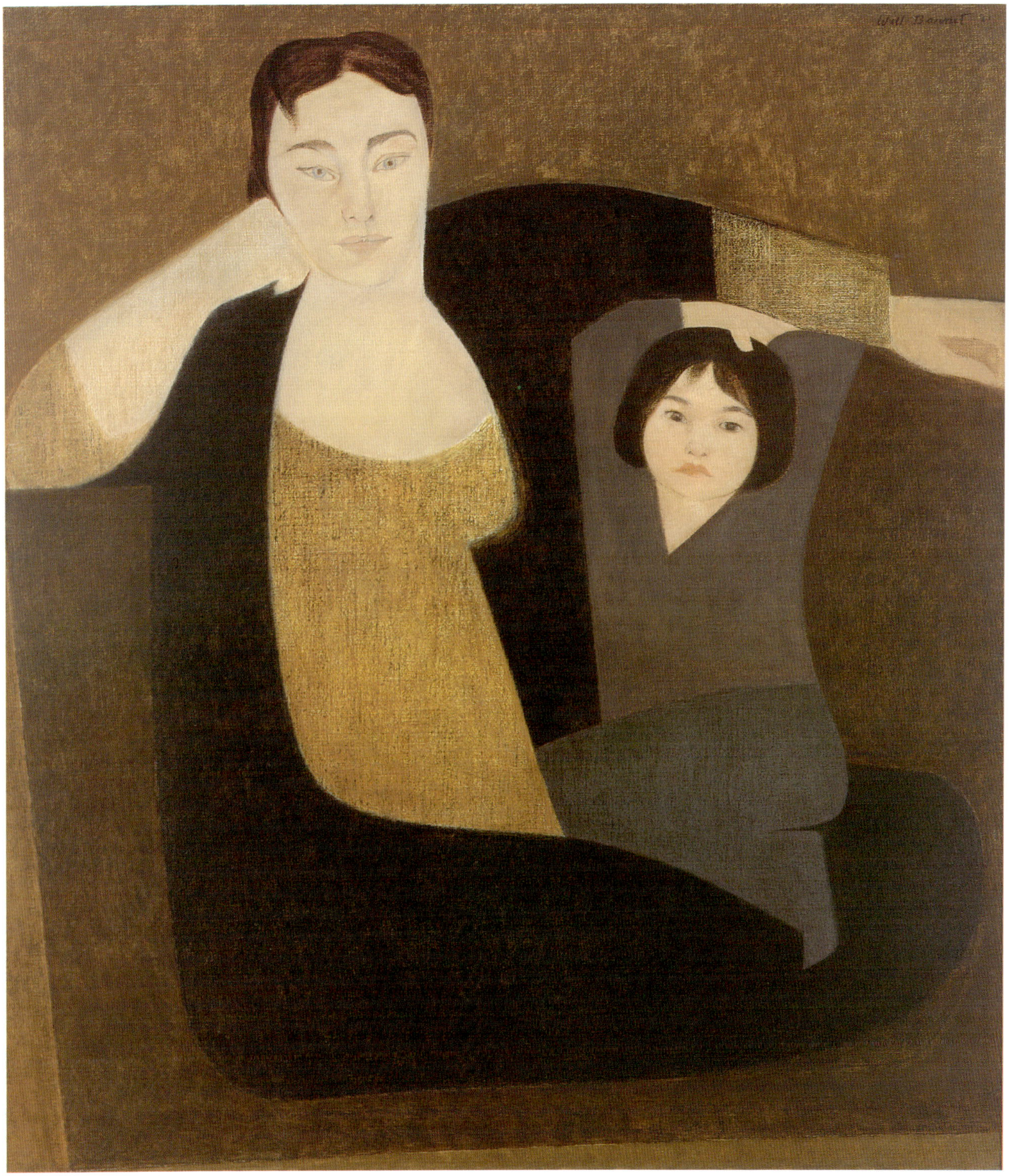

Cat. no. 1. *Mother and Child*, 1961.

then switches behind the head to the inner track that curves around the golden tunic. As this line trails off near the child's toes, a small wedge opening between the girl's heels and hindquarters briefly picks up its horizontal reach before spilling into the eastern-most expanse of the dark robe's gathers.

The child's raised arms parallel the inclination of her mother's; the right one angles just enough to harmonize with the neckline that dips a bit lower to the left. Just beneath the crisp edge of the mother's dark sleeve, a single finger slips from the clasped hands, initiating a movement through similarly-shaped bangs down the side of her face. The adjacent v-neck points the way further down, to the zig-zag that locks child and mother together. It is in this region that the eye most readily recognizes the flat and independent—the *abstract*—quality of the forms that comprise this painting. More hard-edged shapes than torsos or legs, they exhibit no chiaroscuro to bestow any sense of depth, and with each, anatomical accuracy is freely sacrificed for the sake of design. A pentimento near the woman's breast indicates that its size has been reduced, perhaps to limit its reference, or perhaps to grant greater authority to the adjoining dark segment. More likely it was diminished to conform to the contrapuntal decrescendo of curvilinear forms that flows from the lower right, from the edge of the robe, through the child's derriere to the breast, and then up to the mother's chin. The absence of linear or atmospheric perspective maximizes such movement by holding the forms as close as possible to the picture plane. No longer inhibited by artificial conventions, spaces normally confined to supporting roles now yield shapes—in this instance, those on either side of the child—that participate as equal elements in the painting's construction.

Mitigating the influence of the third dimension in his painting had long been for Barnet far more important than deciding whether to limit the referential properties of his forms. He first voiced such notions in a short essay published in 1950 titled "Painting without Illusion."[15] The argument is certainly modern, falling well within the parameters of abstraction as it was generally practiced at the time. Given what we know of his work later in the decade, this should come as no surprise. He calls for a painterly space independent from the laws of nature, and, in articulating this space, he urges an approach that above all recognizes the tectonic potential inherent in the two-dimensional character of the canvas. "We must realize that the quadrangle on which we draw or paint," he wrote, "has basic dimensions and movements. It moves structurally according to its basic architecture, and the artist builds with the horizontal and vertical within the quadrangle's architecture."[16]

What *is* a bit startling with this article, however, is that to illustrate the text, rather than selecting one of his own recent paintings, or for that matter, any work remotely connected to modernism, Barnet placed a thirteenth-century Florentine Madonna and Child (fig. 3). As might be expected, given the overall tone of the essay, the panel receives a fairly straightforward formal analysis. A good deal of care, for example, is taken to detail how its painterly elements—form, line, and color—relate to one another as they construct a space wholly wedded to the picture plane, and thus beyond the domain of nature. Barnet then concludes the study with a sentence clearly intended to signal precisely where he stood among his contemporaries. He writes, "Nothing is left to chance or illusion."[17]

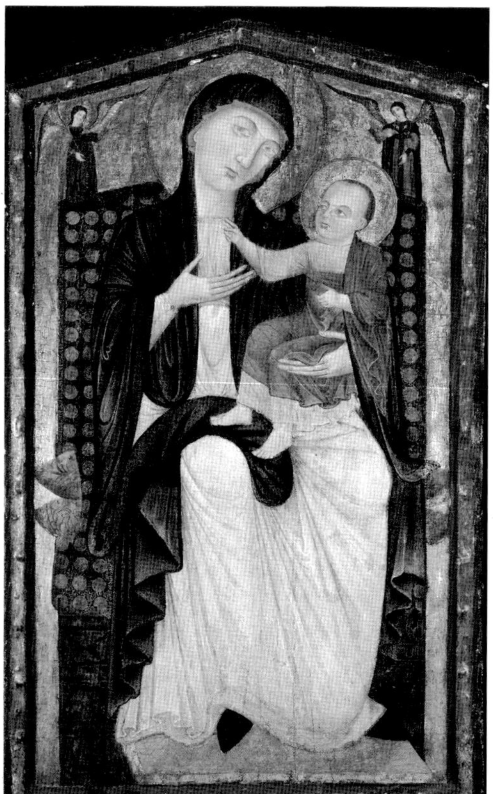

Fig. 3. Artist unknown (Florentine), *Madonna and Child Enthroned*, late thirteenth century. Tempera on wood, gold ground, 60 1/2 x 36 inches. The Metropolitan Museum of Art, Gift of George Blumenthal, 1941. (41.100. 21)

The implication that painting might be accomplished through indiscriminate effort refers, somewhat obliquely, to Abstract Expressionism, which, by the time Barnet published "Painting without Illusion," was well on its way to dominating the art scene in New York. The artists who comprised this group had not quite become "the Irascibles,"[18] but several had already received a good deal of critical attention. Foremost among them in this vein was Jackson Pollock, then well into his drip method, who just a year prior had been the focus of a *Life* feature that asked in its title, "Is he the greatest living painter?"[19] Such recognition could not have gone without notice on the part of Barnet, and he would have been particularly interested in the article's reiteration of an earlier claim by Pollock. "When I am *in* my painting," he is quoted as saying, "I'm not aware of what I'm doing."[20] The apparent willingness to allow an element of chance, or at least a sense of unpredictability, into the process, a disposition shared by many of the artists in the group,[21] might have seemed somewhat cavalier to an artist inclined to approach the canvas in a more disciplined manner. A few years later, in the article he prepared for *The World of Abstract Art*, Barnet specifically took issue with such unfettered expression, suggesting that it signaled "a destruction of traditions and a violation of the laws that govern the visual meaning of painting."[22]

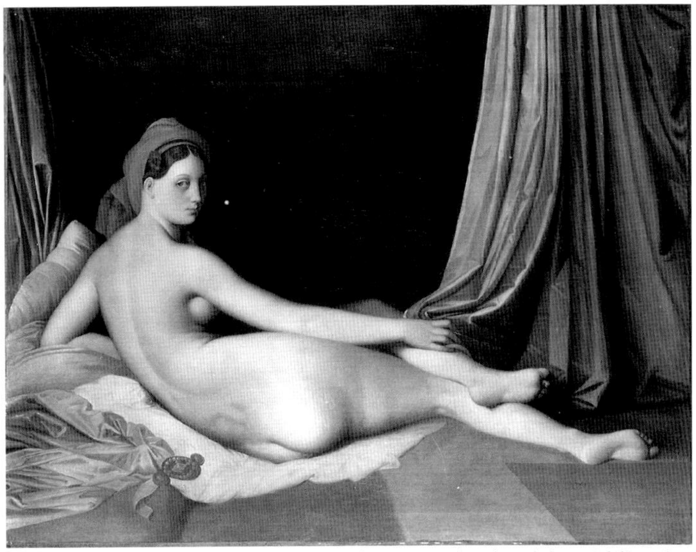

Fig. 4 Jean-Auguste-Dominique Ingres (French, 1780–1867) and Workshop, *Odalisque in Grisaille*, 1824–34. Oil on canvas, 32 3/4 x 43 inches. The Metropolitan Museum of Art, Catharine Lorillard Wolfe Collection, Wolfe Fund, 1938. (38.65)

Barnet was well aware at this point that the traditions of which he spoke were not necessarily embodied in the kind of painting in which the imitation of nature, through the illusion of three-dimensionality, has been preponderant. "I've never had much use for perspective in my own work," Barnet has admitted, "I've always felt that it destroys or in some other way does violence to the picture plane."[23] And indeed, it was toward the Italian primitives that he turned for assistance in his early struggles to comprehend modernism. "It wasn't seeing the work of the modern school of Paris, but looking at Byzantine art and these early Italian painters that led me to the way of working that is indicative of how I see the world on a canvas," he has recently allowed.[24]

> This style of painting taught me about the flat surface I was working with, what kind of language to use to make a real painting. Look at the simplicity and compression of space. It's a flat painting with no real modeling, no attempt to create any illusion, but when you study it, you feel spatial differences. The flat surface has its own space. Every piece of drapery has form, structure, and weight, yet the painting is flat. It doesn't come forward or fall back.[25]

This is not to say that post-Albertian artists could not be appreciated, as long as their use of perspective did not subvert the integrity of the picture plane. In fact, Barnet has expressed admiration for a wide range of artists—Piero della Francesca, Vermeer, Poussin, Chardin—who in one way or another have depended upon Renaissance values in their painting but for whom the sense of design outweighed the three-dimensional essence of their forms. In maintaining a link to these artists, he felt a kinship with the plight of Paul Cézanne, who, in his effort to move beyond the aleatoric vistas of his naturalist colleagues, also turned to the Old Masters for structural guidance.[26] But perhaps the most important model in this instance is Jean-Auguste-Dominique Ingres, hailed by Barnet as "one of the great structuralists and a master of abstraction."[27]

Because of his connection to the *Académie des Beaux-Arts*, which regulated the training of artists in nineteenth-century France, and in particular due to his opposition to the chromatics of Eugène Delacroix, Ingres was considered a Philistine, still in Barnet's day, by those who championed the avant garde, whether their favor rested with Romanticism, Realism, or Impressionism.[28] Barnet recognized, however, that Ingres, unlike his lesser colleagues and countless followers who mistook his insistence upon superior draftsmanship for slavish accuracy in the transcription of nature, practiced an exceedingly liberal form of academism, one in which the role of illusion was often restrained in order to benefit the two-dimensional dynamics of the picture plane. At first glance, a painting such as *Odalisque in Grisaille* (fig. 4), with its crisply delineated fabric and sculptural figure, seems nearly photographic in its verisimilitude. Closer examination tells a different story. The woman's right arm stretches beyond anatomical feasibility to complete the immense curve that initiates with the drapery to the right, and her smoothly arched spine requires several additional vertebrae to accomplish a competing contour. Her left thigh fades into the shadows at an impossible angle, exaggerated in order to harmonize with a series of triangular caverns that traverse the figure in reaction to the opening in the curtains. The distortion allows a proper vector for the legs, which cut a splendid diagonal toward the lower right corner. This movement is brushed horizontally as well by a pattern of fingers and toes (but for the latter only nine in total) and carried further to the right by sympathetic folds at the base of the drapery. At each turn, where the figure is made to conform to the design of the composition, the illusion of real space transitions to the actuality of painterly space.

Part of the appeal of such highly structured work lies in Barnet's own rather traditional education. Between 1928 and 1931, he studied at the School of the Museum of Fine Arts in Boston, where he received an academic training not at all unlike what young artists were afforded a century earlier while studying at the *École des Beaux-Arts* in Paris. He had courses in anatomy, perspective, and color, but drawing provided the foundation: a full year from casts, then at least another year with live models before being allowed to paint. His principal drawing instructor, Philip Leslie Hale, traced his artistic lineage to Ingres, through one of his teachers during his own tenure at the *École*. Barnet appreciated this link to the French master, and for several years he remained content to absorb all that the academic system could offer.[29] A need to come to terms with modernism, however, together with a desire to comprehend more fully the idea of composition, which was not a strong component of the Boston Museum School's curriculum, sent Barnet off to New York to study at the Art Students League. He spent the next ten years attempting to unlearn most of what he had garnered in Boston, but at least one aspect of the School, appropriately modified, remained influential in his work. In a 1962 interview, when asked whether drawing was a significant stage in the realization of a painting, he responded (with more than a hint of what he felt drawing lacked in his own training):

> I think it is major. Of course, we've changed our point of view about drawing since I was a student. Even in those days, however, drawing was not just copying a thing. It was interpreting it from a certain point of view. Today, we interpret from another point of view. Good drawing today means a great facility for the kind of observation which incorporates the whole world. It requires not just descriptive skills but a certain ability to put objects in relation to one another. What I felt as a student was a lack of interrelatedness. We didn't learn how to put things together. One of the errors of that period was that we learned to draw one thing at a time and weren't taught what each thing meant in relation to something else. Drawing today has a much wider meaning—the ability to give things relatedness.[30]

The shift in the point of view addressed here by Barnet, from drawing a single figure to including an ensemble of objects in one's sketch, actually reflects a desire to return to an aspect that was very much a part of the nineteenth-century curriculum. Toward the end of their drawing program, students enrolled with the French *Académie* during Ingres' lifetime were regularly assigned problems in composition, and they were additionally encouraged to develop compositional notes, called *croquis*, which could be utilized later in the realization of a painting.[31] The very notion of introducing invention to the drawing stage has in fact been basic to the academic tradition since its origin, which predates the French system by 100 years. During the late sixteenth century, Giorgio Vasari helped to lay the foundations of the *Accademia del Disegno* in Florence by bringing the three arts—painting, sculpture, and architecture—together under the single

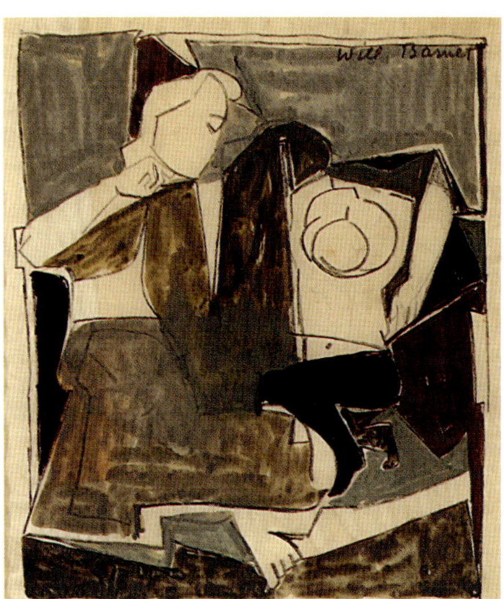

Cat. no. 4. Study for *Mother and Child*, 1960.

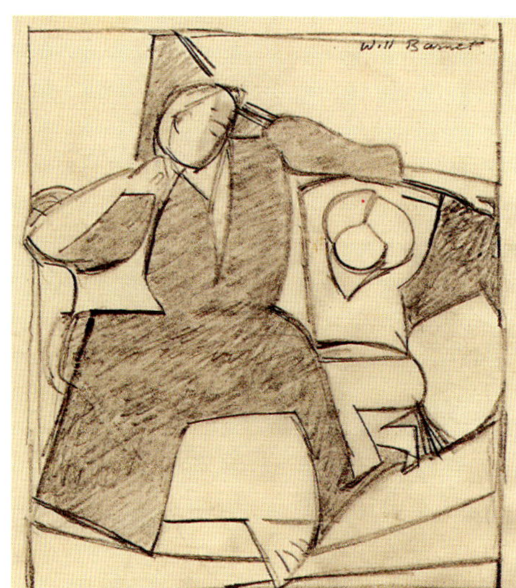

Cat. no. 5. Study for *Mother and Child*, 1960–61.

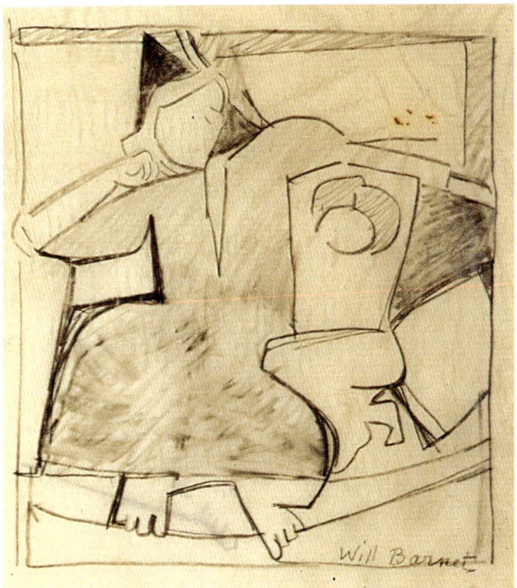

Cat. no. 7. Study for *Mother and Child*, c. 1960.

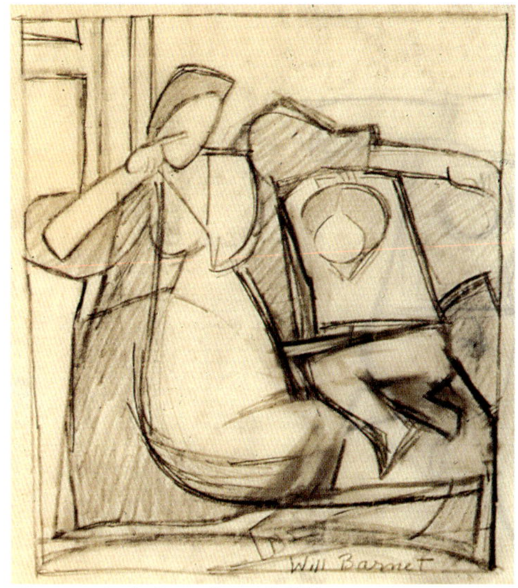

Cat. no. 8. Study for *Mother and Child*, c. 1960.

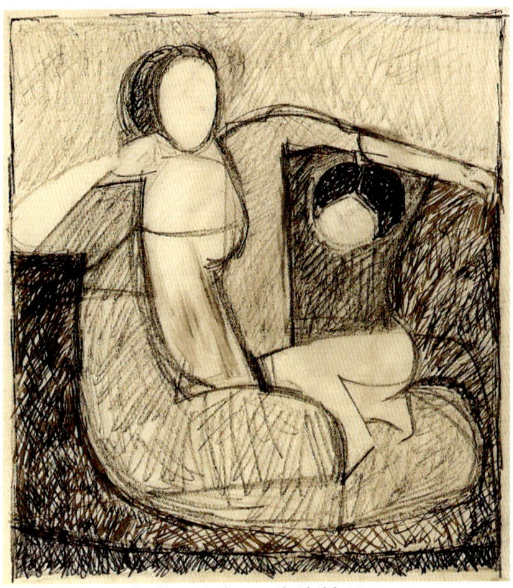

Cat. no. 9. Study for *Mother and Child*, 1960–61.

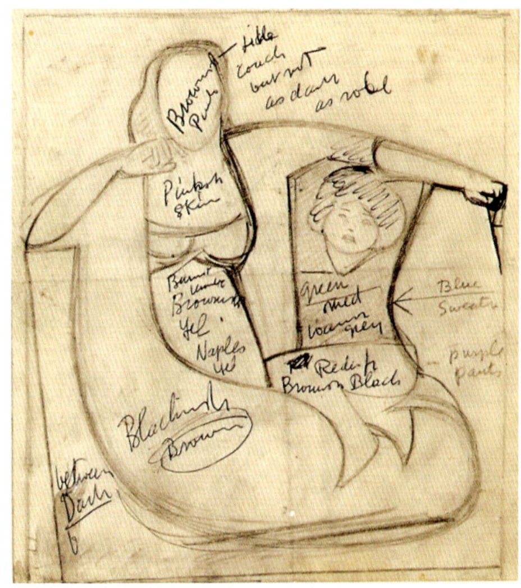

Cat. no. 11. Study for *Mother and Child*, 1960.

principle of *disegno*, which he identified as "a visual expression and clarification of that concept which one has in the intellect, and that which one imagines in the mind, and builds up in the idea."[32] This was a key distillation of Renaissance thought, which saw *disegno*—that is, drawing—not as the immediate imitation of things experienced, but as the first and most significant manifestation of an *idea*. Drawing was thus understood as a measure not of facility, but of intellect.

For Barnet, drawing, specifically as it relates to the notion of *disegno*, figures indispensably in the creative process. In realizing *Mother and Child* (following a procedure identical to the one employed to produce the preceding abstract work), he generated hundreds of sketches over an entire year before transferring his ideas to canvas. The drawings represent two distinct stages in the development of the design. With the first set (cat. nos. 4, 5, and 7), Barnet concentrated on abstracting the figures into angular components within a design in which the displacement and balance of mass appears to be the primary force. A relatively fair amount of referential detail remains to play a structural role, including the mother's feet, a pillow on the sofa, and—in an appropriate promotion of negative space—an asymmetrical opening in a pair of curtains behind the woman's head. A studio window lingers in a related sketch (cat. no. 8), which, because of the more rounded features now defining the mother's gown, might be considered transitional. The second group of drawings (cat. nos. 9, 11, and 12), offering softer forms and a fluid and more linear movement, comes closer in composition to the painting. It is thus feasible to impute a slightly later chronology to these studies; however, several elements from the earlier set found their way into the painting as

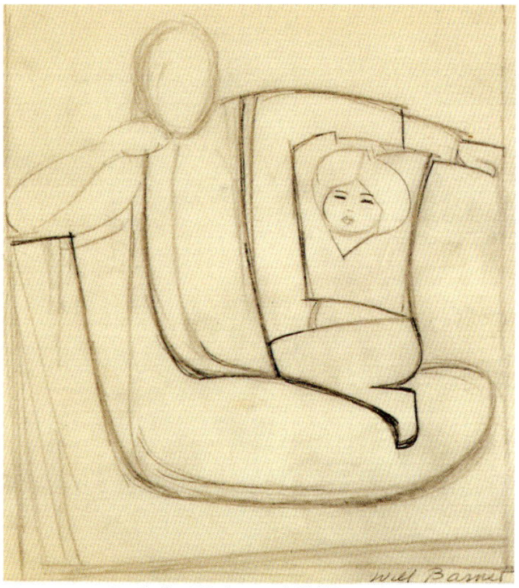

Cat. no. 12. Study for *Mother and Child*, 1960.

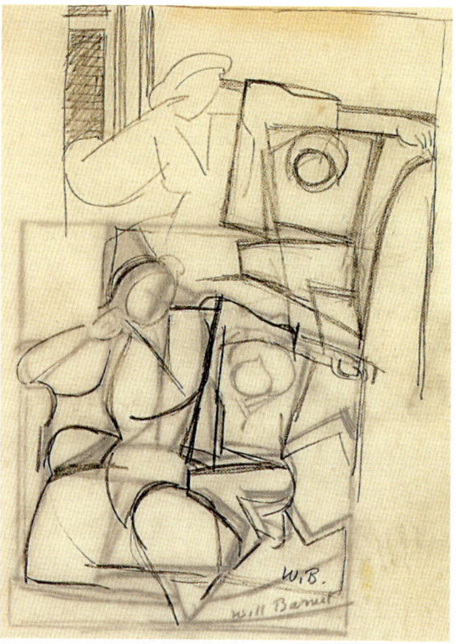

Cat. no. 6. Study for *Mother and Child*, 1960–61.

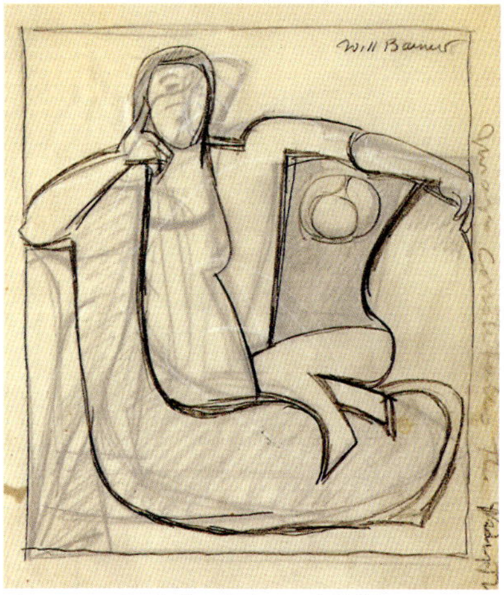

Cat. no. 10. Study for *Mother and Child*, c. 1960.

well. The slender wedge expanding across the base, for example, occurs only in the first group. And the coloring filled into one of the first studies (cat. no. 4) represents a harmony far closer to the painting than any of the color indications from the later group (cat. no. 11).

Within each set the size of the drawings remains remarkably similar. Most have been executed on tracing paper, which allowed Barnet to rapidly reproduce a successful sketch for further working simply by placing one sheet atop another, or, as in the case of two drawings in this exhibition (cat. nos. 6 and 10), by folding over an unused portion of the same sheet.[33]

Perhaps the most fascinating aspect of the drawings for *Mother and Child* is that within them can be found the genesis of another closely related, yet quite abstract painting. The second group of studies in particular appears to have stimulated the path toward further reduction. In one of the abridged sketches (cat. no. 20), the woman's arms have joined with her robe to create a single form that, angling upward in the lower right, strongly emphasizes the protective nature of the mother in the painting. The interior portions of the mother's figure, however—as a similar drawing, the first of two on a single sheet (cat. no. 21), makes clear—have been divorced to interact instead with the child's domain. In the second image of this sheet, the enveloping form melds with the remaining outer space (formerly representing the wall behind the couple and the sofa in which they rested) while the images now associated with the child consolidate within a chrysalitic pocket. The womb-like nature of this hollow becomes evident in further studies (cat. no. 22), in which the surrounding component approaches its final shape.

The resulting painting, suitably titled *Enclosure* (cat. no. 18), was initially colored bluish black against a golden ocher and left unfinished in 1962. In 2003, Barnet revisited the composition, completing it with the current harmony of soft olive and matte black versus a blue adulterated with enough white to successfully reverse its receding tendencies. The new complexion, aided immeasurably by the advancing light blue, creates an optical resonance that amplifies the uneven but undeniable centripetal force of the internal figure. The image pushes mostly to the left as it coils counterclockwise, rocking the enclosing form just enough off axis to match the angle of the abstracted couch in *Mother and Child*, which, of course, was part of the original source for the gesture.[34]

As the evolution of *Enclosure* demonstrates, Barnet continued to generate abstract ideas in the early 1960s; however, such efforts were for the most part an anomaly, at least for a few years. The principal reason behind his turn toward a more realistic approach involved, in fact, a desire to break from abstraction in order to replenish his imagination.[35] Thus, between 1961 and 1963, with every intention of eventually returning to the style that produced *Singular Image* and *Big Duluth*, Barnet sought momentary respite, beginning with *Mother and Child*, in paintings that embraced the referential qualities of the human figure. An overwhelming majority of these canvases featured various arrangements of just his wife, daughter, and family cat, creating over a two-year period a rather cohesive and remarkably attractive set of variations on a theme.

One of the more successful of these variations is *The Blue Robe* (cat. no. 26), which, like *Mother and Child*, features a wealth of anatomical liberties that allow the figures to conform to a composition easily more symphonic than transcriptive in nature. Although nearly square (just four inches wider than tall), the painting *feels* abundantly horizontal, due in a large part to the accentuation of the three underlying rectangular bands at each juncture by limbs stretching in either direction. The woman's right arm is especially dynamic, reaching from as far back as her left shoulder across the entire width of the canvas. Together with the equally forceful weight of her left arm, which anchors the entire right side with the resolve of a Doric column, the woman outlines the parameters of the painting's action. A series of diagonals further delineates this space; the most visible follows the straight edge of the robe that parallels the woman's left arm. The others are more subtle: the short line of the torso between breast and cat; the edge of the breast as it emerges from the robe (and which catches up again below, in the child's lap); the eye contact between mother and daughter; and the slope of the woman's legs beneath the robe, further to the left.

Although seemingly innocuous, these oblique lines play a significant role in the reading of *The Blue Robe*. The outer two define the realm of the child in terms of the mother, thus preparing the stage for graphically relating one to the other while the figures themselves, as in *Mother and Child*, remain for the most part physically isolated from one another. The mountainous triangle composed of the reclining child and the mother's flexed legs, for example, would not otherwise be feasible. Additionally, the diagonals converge, almost like flat orthogonals, several inches above the picture frame, at a point precisely where the woman's head would rest if completely erect. Lowering the head thwarts the vertical tendencies of this confluence. But the gesture is also kinetic. Confined now within an impossibly narrow band, the angle of the head, falling to the left, forces the movement to follow the woman's

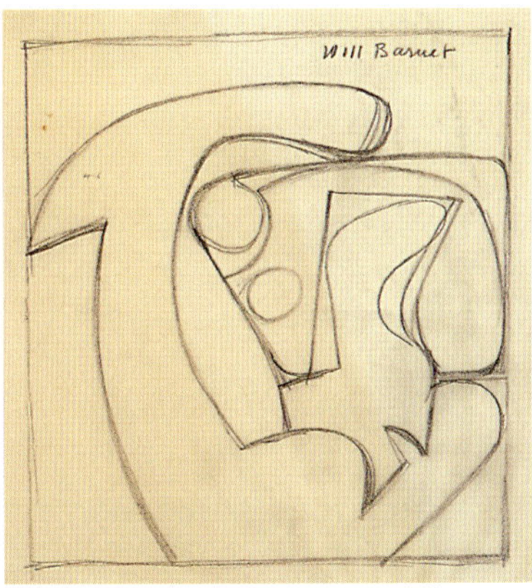

Cat. no. 20. Study for *Mother and Child*, 1960.

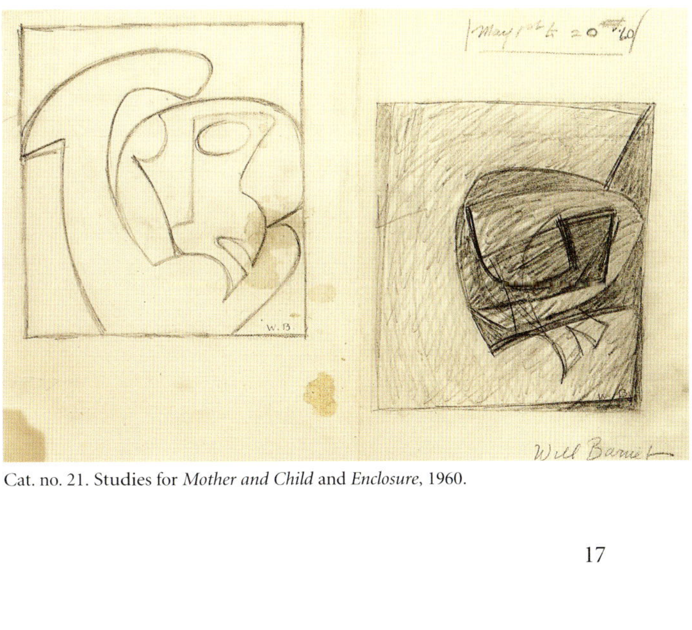

Cat. no. 21. Studies for *Mother and Child* and *Enclosure*, 1960.

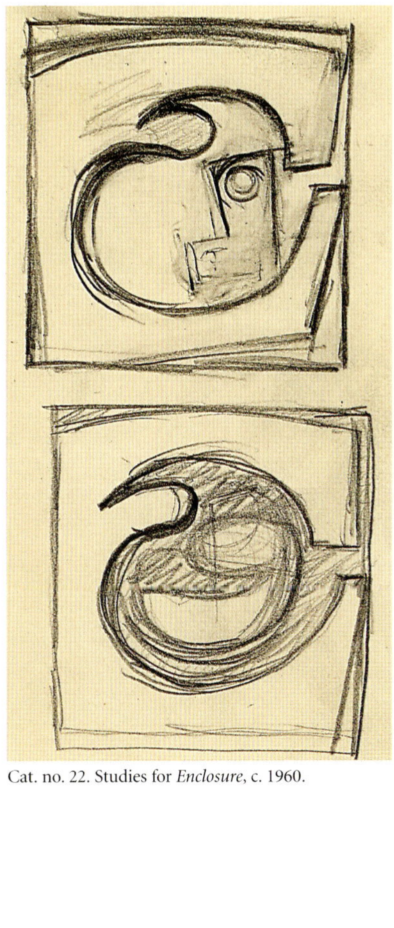

Cat. no. 22. Studies for *Enclosure*, c. 1960.

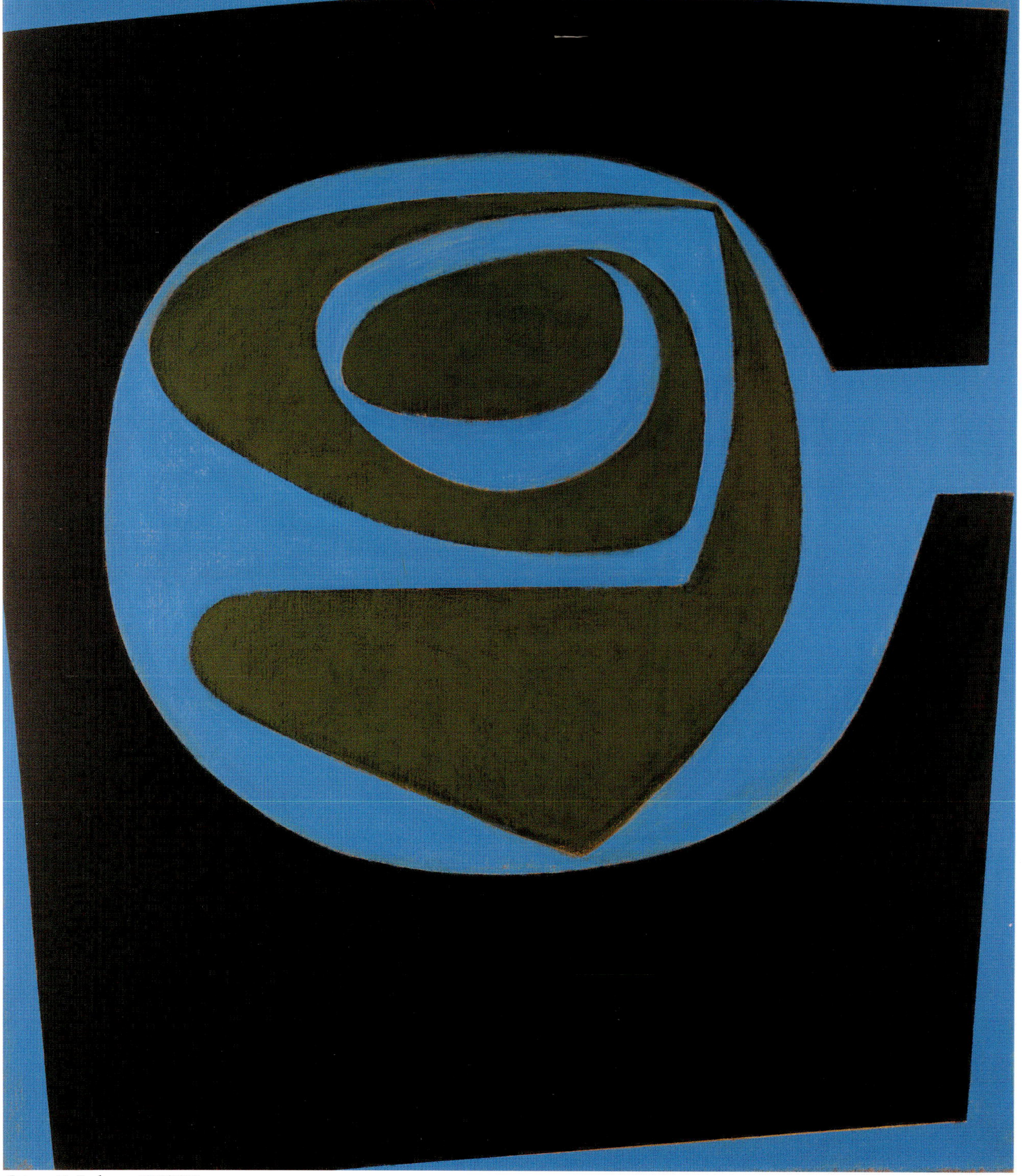

Cat. no. 18. *Enclosure*, 1962/2003.

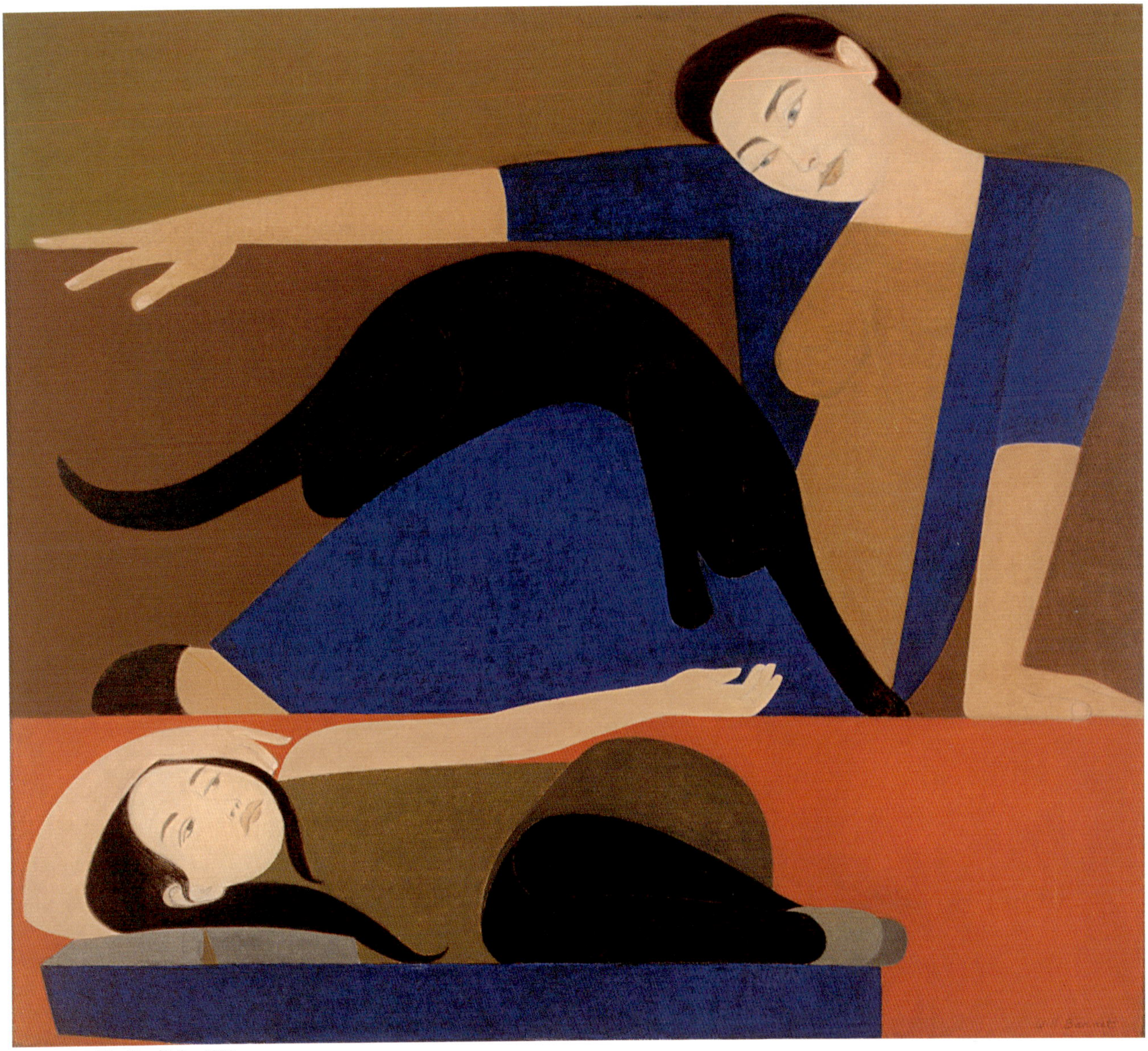

Cat. no. 26. *The Blue Robe*, 1962.

tapering arm across the canvas. The splayed fingers dissipate the energy; however the perfectly poised index finger loops around to the bowing tail of the cat, the first element in a rolling feline arabesque that directs the eye back toward the woman and then down her lap. One of the cat's forelegs continues the flow to the right, where it meets an abrupt halt at the intersection of the aforementioned robe diagonal and a staid block of orange-red in the lowest horizontal segment. The other leg, though, joins with the robe's right edge in a competing oblique thrust toward the child's hand. In tandem with this motion, a cascade of more gentle forms, initiated with the woman's nod, descends from the right breast through the cat's similarly-shaped head to be caught as well by the child. This hand becomes a critical focal point for directing nearly all of the movement generated above into the lower region, passing in part down the one arm and around the child's head with the other, and then off to the right with the flow of her hair. Yet because of an expertly crafted thumb (and the line of the breast above), the eye jumps as well across the wrist and into the girl's lap, where it follows the rapid diminuendo of her gathered legs. The child's hair, styled to resound sympathetically with the cat's tail, captures a bit of this action to commence a contrapuntal line that retrogresses, with the assistance of a subtle but significant lift of her appropriately angled mat in the lower left, along the same path, circumnavigating her head to gain access once again to the center of the canvas.

The initial drawings for *The Blue Robe* reveal that finding a means of addressing the lower third of the painting had been a concern for the artist since its conception. One of the very first sketches (cat. no. 27) features just the mother and cat; the latter is posed in the opposite direction, with its tail falling over the edge of the sofa. As the studies progressed to include the child (cat. no. 29), Barnet thought this dangling tail might provide a way of connecting the two human figures. This idea endured even as the mother approached her final form (cat. no. 30), and dissipated in favor of the current design only after a series of sketches involving the extension of the cat's paws (cat. no. 35) proved to be a more engaging motif.

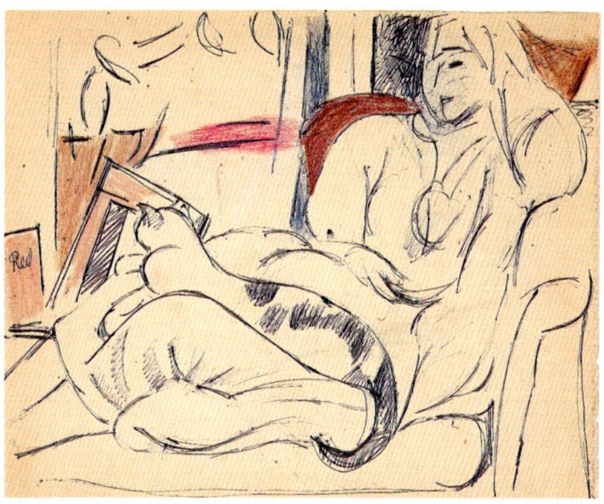

Cat. no. 27. Study for *The Blue Robe*, c. 1960.

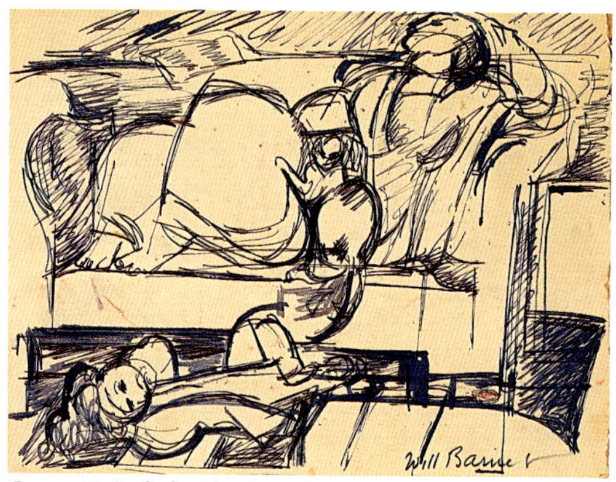

Cat. no. 29. Study for *The Blue Robe*, c. 1960.

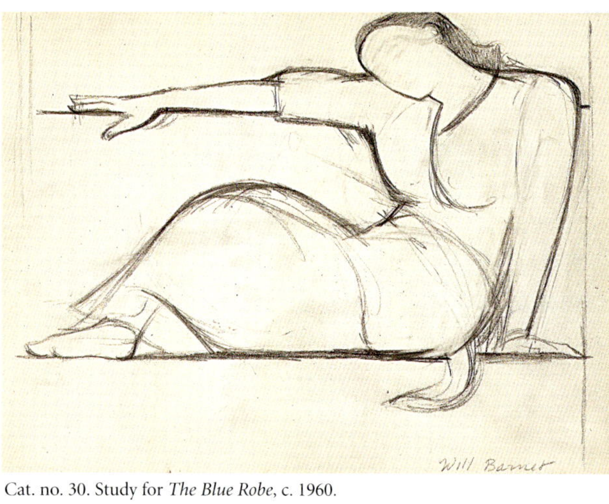

Cat. no. 30. Study for *The Blue Robe*, c. 1960.

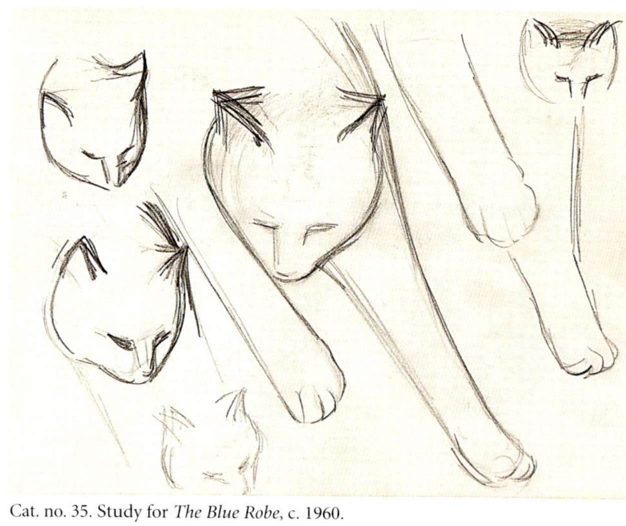

Cat. no. 35. Study for *The Blue Robe*, c. 1960.

For the summer of 1963, less than a year following the completion of *The Blue Robe*, Barnet accepted a teaching position at the University of Washington in Spokane. The western venue, and in particular the expansive topography of eastern Washington, rekindled an interest in landscape and, with it, the kind of monumental abstraction he had purposefully abandoned several years earlier.[36] Upon returning to New York, during the fall and into the early months of 1964, he began to distill his response to the Spokane environs in two distinct series of paintings. As he did with works such as *Big Duluth*, Barnet synthesized much of what affected him—trees, mountains, the desert—into highly reductive compositions effectively purged of all immediate reference. In one of the uncharacteristically few drawings for the larger series, however (cat. no. 44), scored in red pencil for transfer to a canvas never realized (although a similar image very close in scale later materialized as a hand-colored etching; see cat. no. 49), he offers in the color indications some clues to the originating imagery. The gently curved banner derives from clouds observed in a sky almost as big as in nearby Montana, and the sharply angular conglomeration in the center, marked simply "Black Falls," comes in part from a spectacular cascade Barnet experienced not far from Spokane.[37] The "arm" is another enclosing gesture, probably rooted in the vegetation surrounding the falls,[38] but now a purely painterly element employed to hold the explosive nature of the spikes in check.[39]

Barnet's initial inclination with this design was to extend it horizontally to match the endless expanse of nature he observed around Spokane (cat. no. 45).[40] He often employs the analogy of an elastic band to illustrate his intention, pulling it in both directions to reach its optimal strength, just at the breaking point.[41] In the resulting painting, titled *Great Spokane* and finished in 1965, this effort reached the nearly panoramic width of eight feet. Having succeeded in this direction, Barnet decided to explore the idea's vertical limits in *Eden* (cat. no. 40), begun in 1964 and completed the following year. The selection of a single spike, perhaps the only practical solution to the challenge, posed difficulties not encountered in the horizontal version. There, the effect of raising the composition with a wedge waxing toward the lower right—a gesture employed often by Barnet (and present in all four paintings featured in the exhibition) to generate tension or movement—is not so traumatic, spread as it is over a relatively great distance. In *Eden*, the truncated width accelerates the incline, forcing the one peak perilously to the left. It is caught, of course, by the embracing arm; however, its latch, now compressed within an unfamiliarly narrow space, threatens structural imbalance. The resolution, already suggested in the watercolor study (cat. no. 42) but most evident in the painting, rests with

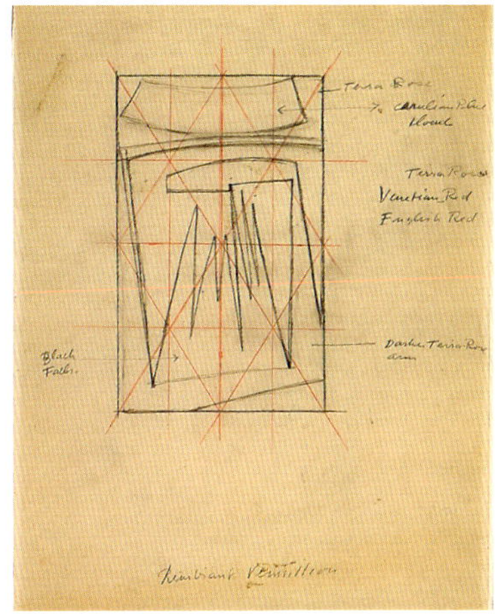

Cat. no. 44. Study for Spokane series, c. 1964.

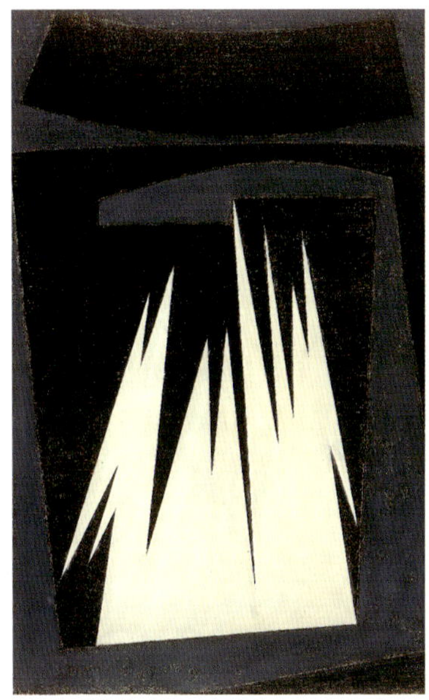

Cat. no. 49. *Spokane*, c. 1965.

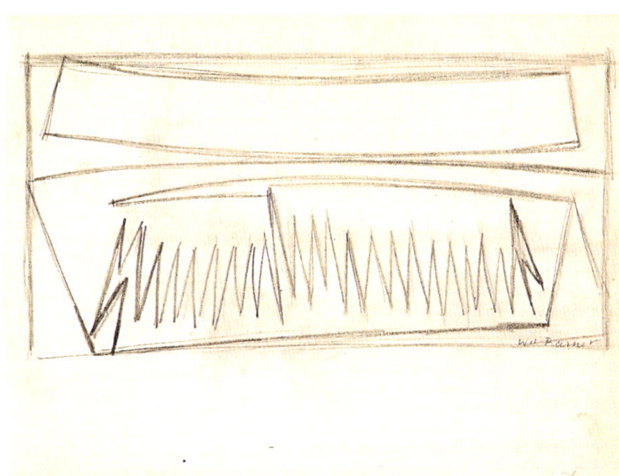

Cat. no. 45. Study for Spokane series, c. 1964.

the cloud-like form above. Billowing slightly as it passes impossibly close to the horizon line (causing the latter to bow slightly upward in response), its center of gravity shifts to the right, adding just enough counterweight to return the composition to stasis.

Because of its title, some scholars have been encouraged to read *Eden* in somewhat transcendental terms, thus linking Barnet to a tradition in American painting that includes artists such as Thomas Cole, Marsden Hartley, Arthur Dove, and Mark Rothko.[42] There is, however, a purely personal aspect to consider as well. While working on the Spokane series during the fall of 1963, Barnet vividly remembers hearing about the assassination of John F. Kennedy, a president for whom he had the highest regard. Kennedy's death affected him deeply, forging a sense of melancholy that surfaced a year later in the dark tones of a smaller version of *Eden* titled *Black Spokane* (cat. no. 41). The feeling lingered with the completion of *Eden*, which signals in its antithetical colors the hope for a better world yet to come.[43]

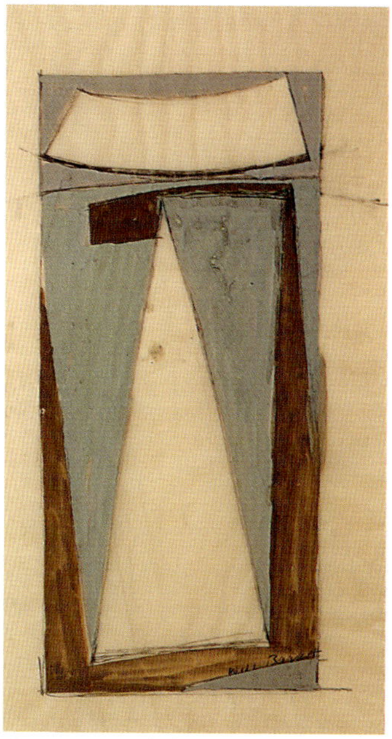

Cat. no. 42. Study for *Eden*, c. 1964.

With the Spokane series Barnet felt he had successfully navigated a return to the abstraction of the late 1950s.[44] In the spring of 1965, as if to emphasize the reconciliation (and ostensibly to place his figural diversion fully behind him as well), he showed nine of the Spokane paintings together with eight canvases from the Duluth period in an exhibition at Grippi & Waddell Gallery.[45] The catalogue further stressed the connection by featuring a contemporaneous photograph of the artist poised before *Singular Image*. The impression, however, was short lived. *Eden* and the other Spokane works completed in 1965 were the last abstract paintings of his career.[46] Barnet began to realize that canvases such as *Mother and Child* and *The Blue Robe*, far from momentary distractions, in fact represented a major breakthrough. Part of the revelation stemmed from the recognition that in the mid-1960s his environment had changed. He was spending more time with his family and colleagues in the New York City area, and this had a profound effect on his work, as though the human figure and the imagery surrounding it became the center of a new landscape for him to observe and assimilate.[47] In reference to his first portrait of Roy Neuberger (fig. 5), dated 1965, Barnet says:

> I painted him sitting in a chair and I tried to give the feeling of a man who makes big decisions. The painting has a bigness about it, I tried to give the feeling of enormous forms. Actually, I

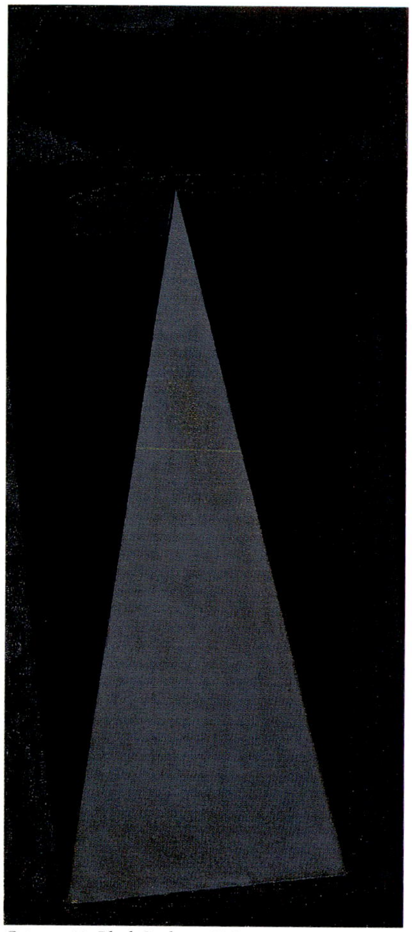

Cat. no. 41. *Black Spokane*, 1964.

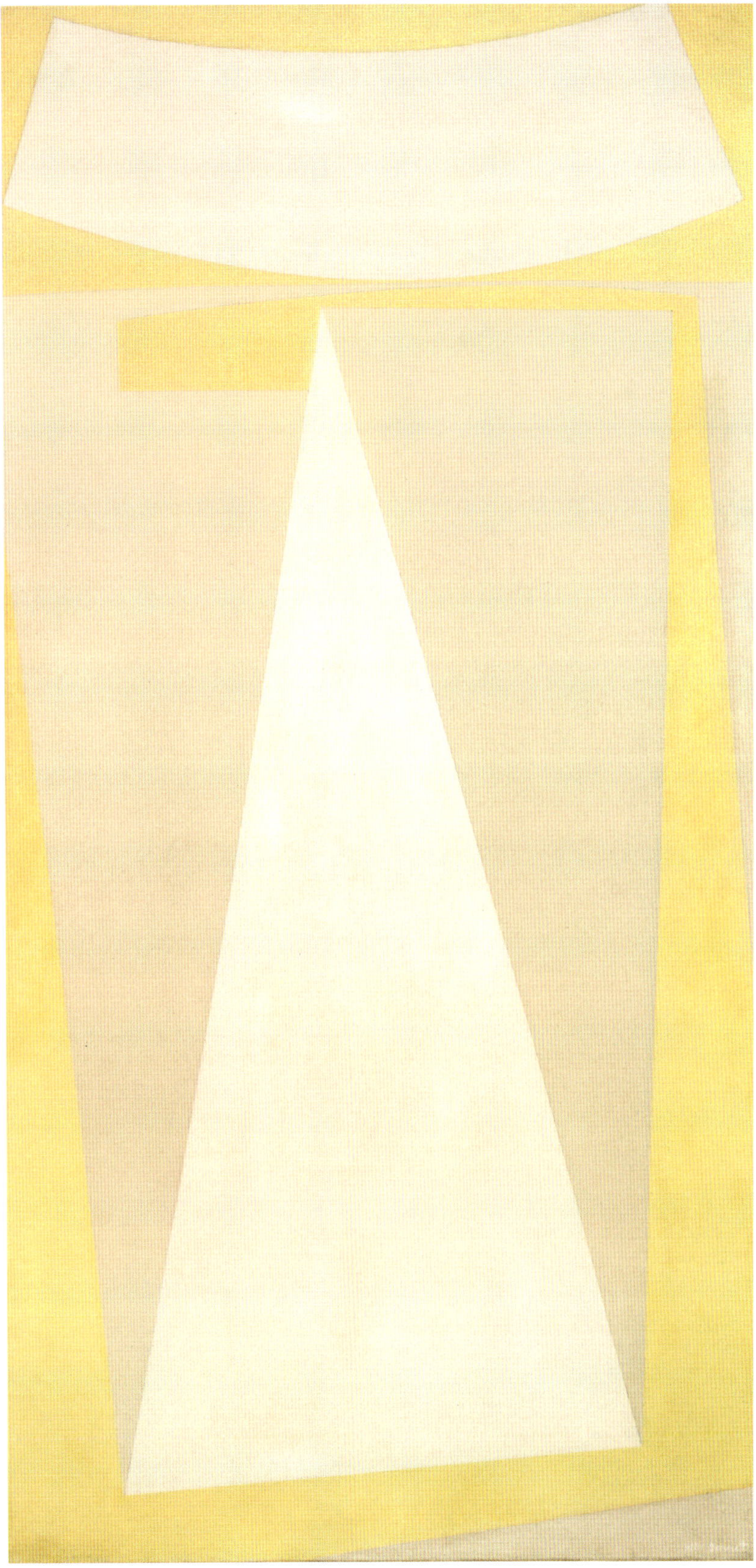

Cat. no. 40. *Eden*, 1964–65.

was trying to reach a climax of ideas where I try to associate myself with the concept Titian had, that the world was a big thing. You know, he made people into mountains. I was trying to make people into mountains. In other words, I was trying to focus on man today being the most important thing again.[48]

In the painting, Barnet imbued Neuberger with a presence larger than life by matching the chair's soaring verticals with corresponding alignments in the right lapel of the overcoat and the crossed legs. Poised slightly off-center, the sitter garners his mountainous shape mostly from the strong, counterbalancing diagonal that links left hand to head. Here we notice that the subject is viewed not quite frontally, but at an angle. The side of the chair, rather than being rendered in accordance with Renaissance perspective, rotates forward to rest parallel with the picture plane, bestowing additional weight, and greater compositional intrigue, to the right portion of the canvas. The left hand and head follow suit to endow a non-illusory sense of mass to both.[49] Barnet considers the comprehension of such formal disposition to be critical in reading his work, whether figural or abstract, for, in a sense, the passion dedicated to rigorously arranging the surface of the canvas supercedes the actual subject as the painting's content. "There's a certain intensity in manipulating the forms into a particular structure," he says.

I experience a great deal of excitement when a painting comes off correctly; when, for example, the expansion of one form relates well to the extension of another. When I can make the structure fit in this way, when the whole thing comes together, I feel as though the painting has transcended life, has gone beyond the idea of just the visual aspects of the model, and become art. In this context you could say that the feelings I experienced in the making of a painting are very much a part of its meaning.[50]

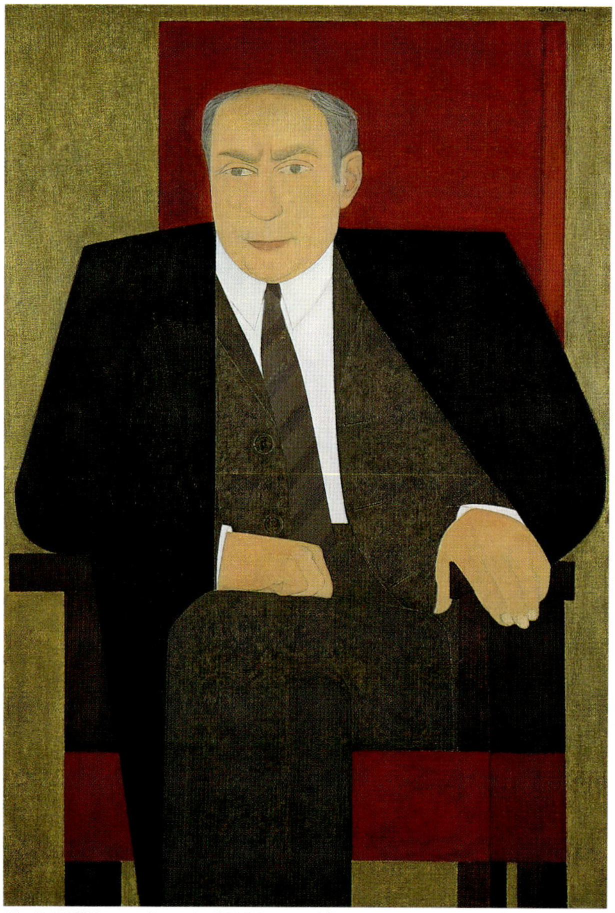

Fig. 5. Will Barnet, *Portrait of RNN*, 1965. Oil on canvas, 67 x 43 inches. Grey Art Gallery, New York University Art Collection, Gift of Roy Neuberger, 1966.13.

In February of 1966, in an about-face from his show the previous year, Barnet presented sixteen relatively referential paintings—including *Mother and Child*, *The Blue Robe*, the Neuberger canvas, and *Remi* (fig. 6), which, outside of family depictions, was his first portrait of the period—again at Grippi & Waddell.[51] The catalogue listed the entries chronologically between 1961 and 1965, with at least one work to represent each year, providing thus a continuum of figural pieces that offered no intimation of concurrent abstract work. As a statement, Barnet reprised a slightly edited version of the one that accompanied his 1962 Bertha Schaefer exhibition, a portion of which bears repeating here:

> My interest has been in developing further the plastic convictions that have been evolving in my abstract paintings; so that a portrait, while remaining a portrait, becomes in this sense an abstraction: the *idea* of a person in its most intense and essential aspect.

These words would become the guiding principle in Barnet's painting for the next thirty-five years, a period during which the *idea* that he speaks of here remained central to every canvas he produced. Abstraction, on the level of *Eden* or *Enclosure*, ceased to be an issue. Indeed, it may be more to the point to say that abstraction per se had never really been an issue, for Barnet has always recognized that in painting the idea—rather than transcribing its physical embodiment in nature—he was adhering to what he perceived to be the most critical aspect of Western painting since its inception.

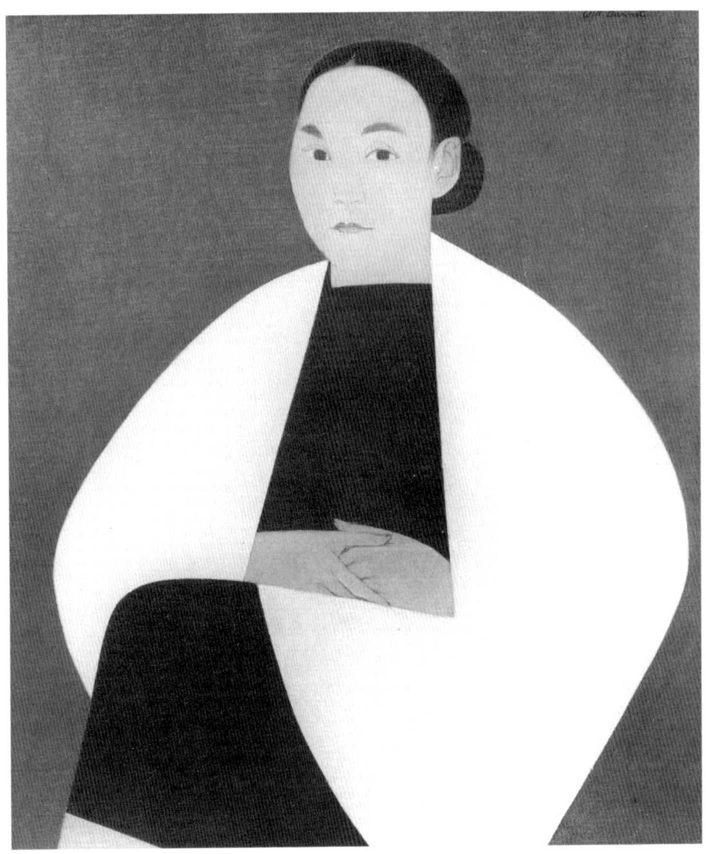

Fig. 6. Will Barnet, *Remi*, 1962. Oil on canvas, 31 x 26 inches. Private collection, New York.

Endnotes

Foreword:

[1] The *Compression–Spokane* edition, numbering 20, was pulled in 1967. See Sylvan Cole, ed., *Will Barnet: Etchings, Lithographs, Woodcuts, Serigraphs, 1932–1972* (New York: Associated American Artists, 1972), n.p., no. 132.

[2] From a January 21, 1974, letter to Will's son, Peter Barnet, and published in the latter's Ed.D. dissertation titled "Will Barnet: Artist and Teacher" (New York: New York University, 1975), pp. 169–71.

[3] Quoted from a letter to Will Barnet dated January 21, 1965, in the *Will Barnet Papers*, Archives of American Art, Smithsonian Institution, microfilm reel 68–22.

Essay:

[1] Quoted here from a clipping from the *Christian Science Monitor*, February 13, 1960, in *Will Barnet Papers*, Archives of American Art, Smithsonian Institution, microfilm reel 69–126.

[2] Lawrence Campbell, "Will Barnet," *Art News*, vol. 58, no. 10 (February 1960), p. 13.

[3] Bennet Schiff, "In the Art Galleries . . .," *New York Post*, February 14, 1960, p. M12. Clipping in *Will Barnet Papers*, Archives of American Art, Smithsonian Institution, microfilm reel 69–126.

[4] Reported by Gail Stavitsky in the exhibition catalogue *Will Barnet: A Timeless World* (Montclair: Montclair Art Museum, 2000), p. 30. It should be noted that the exhaustive research evidenced in Stavitsky's essay, easily the most comprehensive overview of Barnet's work since Robert Doty's 1984 monograph (see note 6), has been the initial source for many of the resources consulted in this study.

[5] Will Barnet, personal notes, 1960s; recorded in Peter Barnet, *Will Barnet: Artist and Teacher*, Ed.D. dissertation (New York: New York University, 1975), p. 86.

[6] Barnet's Duluth experiences have been detailed in a number of studies, including Robert Doty, *Will Barnet* (New York: Harry N. Abrams, 1984), pp. 57–60; Paul Cummings, "Oral History Interview with Will Barnet, Painter and Teacher," Archives of American Art, Smithsonian Institution, January 15, 1968, typescript, pp. 56–59; Emily Goldstein, "A Conversation with Will Barnet," in *Will Barnet: Early Works on Paper*, exhibition catalogue (East Hampton: Glenn Horowitz Bookseller, 1997), p. 14; and Stavitsky, p. 31.

[7] Thomas Messer, introduction to *Will Barnet*, exhibition catalogue (Boston, Institute of Contemporary Art, 1961), n. p. [pp. 3–4].

[8] In fact, the review by Rita Jean Dunn in Barnet's hometown newspaper, *Beverly Evening Times*, makes no mention of the painting ("Will Barnet Exhibit at Contemporary Art Inst.," August 15, 1961). Robert Taylor, in *The Boston Sunday Herald* ("Solo Show Limns Moods of Barnet," August 27, 1961, p. 6B), writes of the late 1950s paintings, "They are among the finest abstractions of our day." He then adds immediately, with no apparent concern over the new direction *Mother and Child* suggests, "As if erecting the capstone, the final painting is a sumptuous portrait of a mother and child, which joins Barnet's pregoing themes. It is masterly." Both citations in *Will Barnet Papers*, Archives of American Art, Smithsonian Institution, microfilm reel 68–22.

[9] There were five abstract canvases featured as well in this exhibition.

[10] Bertha Schaefer Gallery, "New Oils by Will Barnet at Bertha Schaefer Gallery," press release, in *Will Barnet Papers*, Archives of American Art, Smithsonian Institution, microfilm reel 69–126.

[11] Natalie Edgar, "Will Barnet," *Art News*, vol. 60, no. 10 (February 1962), p. 18.

[12] Brian O'Doherty, "Art: Painting and Sculpture Displays," *The New York Times*, January 31, 1962, p. 23.

[13] American Abstract Artists, ed., *The World of Abstract Art* (New York: G. Wittenborn, [1957?]). This edition is not dated; however, more than half of the individual articles are, and all are ascribed to 1956, suggesting that much of the work on the book was completed during this year, in conjunction with AAA's twentieth anniversary. A virtually identical version of *The World of Abstract Art* was published in London by Alec Tiranti with the publication date, 1957, clearly indicated.

[14] Will Barnet, "Aspects of American Abstract Painting," in *The World of Abstract Art*, pp. 105–112. The artist dated his article May 1956.

[15] Will Barnet, "Painting without Illusion." *The League Quarterly*, vol. 22, no. 1 (Spring 1950), pp. 8–9.

[16] *Ibid.*, p. 8.

[17] *Ibid.*, p. 9.

[18] In the January 15, 1951, issue of *Life*, there appeared a now-famous photograph (p. 34) of a group of artists, composed mostly of abstract expres-

sionists, over the caption "Irascible Group of Advanced Artists Led Fight Against Show." The photo served as a prelude to a brief mention of a contemporary art competition held at The Metropolitan Museum of Art ("The Metropolitan and Modern Art," pp. 35–38) against which "the irascible 18" had protested.

19 "Jackson Pollock, Is He the Greatest Living Painter in the United States?," *Life*, vol. 27 (August 8, 1949), pp. 42–45.

20 *Ibid.*, p. 45. The statement originated in Jackson Pollock, "My Painting," *Possibilities I*, Winter, 1947/48; reprinted and more accessible in David Shapiro and Cecile Shapiro, *Abstract Expressionism: A Critical Record* (Cambridge: Cambridge University Press, 1990), pp. 356–57.

21 See, for example, the discussion on gesture by Irving Sandler in *The Triumph of American Painting* (New York: Praeger Publishing, 1970), pp. 92–101.

22 W. Barnet, "Aspects of American Abstract Painting," p. 109.

23 Will Barnet, telephone conversation with the author, February 6, 2003.

24 In Linda S. Price, "Points of Perspective," *American Artist*, vol. 61, no. 664 (November 1997), p. 29. The comment was recorded during a tour of The Metropolitan Museum of Art. In this instance Barnet addresses an early thirteenth-century *Madonna and Child* by Berlinghiero Berlinghieri after failing to locate the painting about which he initially intended to speak. The painting he sought is the *Madonna and Child Enthroned* illustrated here.

25 *Ibid.*, pp. 28–29.

26 "I wanted to make of Impressionism something solid and durable, like the art of the museums" (*J'ai voulu faire de l'impressionisme quelque chose de solide et de durable comme l'art des Musées*), if we are to believe Maurice Denis, who quotes the artist in "Cézanne," *L'Occident*, vol. 12 (September 1907), pp. 118–33. This article was reprinted in, and quoted here from Maurice Denis, *Théories, 1890-1910: du symbolisme et de Gauguin vers un nouvel ordre classique*, 4th ed. (Paris: L. Rouart et J. Waterlin, 1920), p. 250. Barnet specifically indicates his desire to maintain a sense of continuity with tradition, much as Cézanne did, in a 1993 interview: "I think [with my art of the fifties and sixties] I was able to merge old culture, tradition, and modern together. Because I never wanted to destroy the modern idea, like Cézanne said he wanted a link between himself and tradition." See Stephen Polcari, "Oral History Interview with Will Barnet," Archives of American Art, Smithsonian Institution, April 9, 1993, p. 19.

27 Price, p. 35.

28 See, for example, John Rewald's monumental *The History of Impressionism* (New York: The Museum of Modern Art), first published in 1946, where, in the first chapter (p. 19), Ingres is depicted as a hopeless conservative: "Unwilling to give a thought to the natural laws of development, unwilling to see in the past anything but the artists he admired, despising Rubens and hence Delacroix, Ingres had clung to his classic ideals without any consideration for, or interest in, the efforts of those who had chosen other roads, never asking himself whether his conceptions were still in accordance with the times."

29 Discussions on Barnet's training can be found in Richard Brown Baker, "Tape Recorded Interview with Will Barnet," Archives of American Art, Smithsonian Institution, February 3 and 17, 1964, typescript, reel 2, pp. 45–59; Cummings, pp. 12–19; and Stavitsky, pp. 9–10.

30 Mary Anne Guitar, "Close-up of the Artist: Will Barnet," in *Famous Artists Magazine*, vol. 11, no. 1 (Autumn 1962), p. 15.

31 See Albert Boime, *The Academy and French Painting in the Nineteenth Century* (London: Phaidon Press, 1971), pp. 34 and 79ff.

32 Quoted from the second (1568) edition of Vasari's *Lives of the Painters* in Erwin Panofsky, *Idea*, trans. Joseph J. S. Peake (Columbia: University of South Carolina Press, 1968), p. 62.

33 Barnet briefly discusses his use of tracing paper and vellum, saying it "allowed me to explore variations on a compositional format without disrupting the original sketch," in Goldstein, p. 17. It is interesting to note that Ingres, too, regularly employed tracing paper for the same purpose. See Marjorie B. Cohen, "Introduction: In Pursuit of Perfection," in *In Pursuit of Perfection: The Art of J.-A.-D. Ingres*, exhibition catalogue (Louisville: The J.B. Speed Art Museum, 1983), pp. 14–18.

34 The identification of *Enclosure* with *Mother and Child* suggests a reorientation of the woodcuts made after the former. The catalogue raisonné of Barnet's prints, edited by Sylvan Cole and titled *Will Barnet: Etchings, Lithographs, Woodcuts, Serigraphs, 1932–1972* (New York: Associated American Artists, 1972), illustrates the first of the two prints, *Enclosure*, with the (reversed) image rotated ninety degrees to the left (no. 126). The second (Cole no. 127), titled *Enveloping Forms*, is similarly illustrated in the comprehensive checklist that accompanies the more recent print retrospective catalogue *Will Barnet: An American Master* (Loretto: The Southern Alleghenies Museum of Art, 1998), p. 32. With the artist's consent, the current exhibition displays *Enveloping Forms*, (cat. no. 25, not illustrated), oriented in the same manner as the painting.

35 Baker, reel 2, p. 102.

36 The artist's Spokane experience is reported briefly in Doty, pp. 60 and 65; P. Barnet, p. 91; and Stavitsky, pp. 31–33.

37 Their name long since forgotten, Barnet describes these falls as a "fantastic waterway with huge forms of water rushing down the whole mountainside" (quoted in Stavitsky, p. 32). He has additionally remarked (in a February 6, 2003, telephone conversation) that these jagged peaks also rep-

resent a visceral response to the barren and rocky desert near Spokane.

[38] W. Barnet, telephone conversation, February 6, 2003.

[39] In a later discussion (February 21, 2003), Barnet allowed that the arm sweeping over the spikes was adapted from the embracing form in *Enclosure*.

[40] W. Barnet, telephone conversation, February 6, 2003.

[41] First quoted, from the artist's personal notes of the 1960s, in P. Barnet, p. 91.

[42] W. Jackson Rushing III, "Will Barnet's 'True Freedom:' Abstraction in Theory and Practice," in *Will Barnet: The Abstract Work* (New York: Tibor de Nagy Gallery, 1998), n.p. [p. 12]; Stavitsky, pp. 32–33. Both authors apply comments specific to *Eden* that rely in part on the general thoughts on Barnet's abstract landscapes offered by Robert M. Doty in *Will Barnet: Selected Abstract Work 1940–1960* (New York: Kennedy Galleries, 1988), n.p. [p. 2].

[43] Will Barnet, telephone conversation with the author, February 26, 2003.

[44] In the interview with Richard Brown Baker (reel 2, p. 102), after discussing the reasons behind his move toward the figure, Barnet says: "Now in [19]64 my work is . . . all abstract again, and I feel that I can do it now because of the very reason that I feel fresh . . . ."

[45] *Will Barnet: New Painting*, March 23 to April 17, 1965.

[46] That is, through 2002. The reworking of *Enclosure* in early 2003 has stimulated a new interest in this direction, and Barnet is currently developing several canvases that introduce a fresh perspective on his abstract work of the mid-1960s.

[47] W. Barnet, telephone conversation, February 6, 2003.

[48] Cummings, p. 71. For additional comments on this portrait, see Stavitsky, pp. 36–37.

[49] This gesture stems from Barnet's admiration of Byzantine painting. In notes recorded during the 1960s, reported by P. Barnet (p. 39), he writes of Byzantine artists: "How did they get a head to be so solid when they don't really model and they don't use sculptural mass, and they don't even give it a light and dark feeling? They pull out the head so that you see more of the sides and top and bottom, and they sometimes bring the back around and show you that."

[50] Will Barnet, telephone conversation with the author, August 8, 2002. These comments stem from a discussion of Ingres, whose preference for form (over color) has led many to consider him as a rather dispassionate artist. "Not so," says Barnet. "The creativity of form has the passion of the white part of the flame. People often talk of the flame's red portion in terms of intensity or passion, as though the red was the hottest. But white in fact is the hotter, the more passionate." Barnet's point is that even in the presumed "coolness"—which is often equated with the color white—of working with form, there can be found an enthusiasm for painting. The flame analogy is cited from an August 19, 1988, interview with Cathy Barnett in Stavitsky, p. 19.

[51] February 15–March 12, 1966.

Exhibition Checklist

1. *Mother and Child*, 1961
Oil on canvas
46 x 39 inches
Signed in upper right: Will Barnet '61
Collection of the artist
Courtesy Alexandre Gallery, New York

2. Study for *Mother and Child*, c. 1960
Graphite and watercolor on paper
7 1/2 x 7 inches (sheet)
5 3/4 x 5 inches (image)
Signed in lower right: Will Barnet
Courtesy Alexandre Gallery, New York

3. Study for *Mother and Child*, c. 1960
Graphite on paper
13 x 17 inches (sheet, folded)
5 3/4 x 5 inches (image)
Signed in lower right: Will Barnet
Courtesy Alexandre Gallery, New York

4. Study for *Mother and Child*, 1960
Graphite and watercolor on paper
5 1/2 x 4 1/2 inches (image)
Signed in upper right: Will Barnet
Courtesy Alexandre Gallery, New York

5. Study for *Mother and Child*, 1960–61
Graphite on paper
5 1/2 x 4 1/2 inches (image)
Signed in upper right: Will Barnet
Courtesy Alexandre Gallery, New York

6. Study for *Mother and Child*, 1960–61
Graphite on paper
8 x 5 inches (image)
Signed in lower right: W.B.
Courtesy Alexandre Gallery, New York
This study folded over:
Study for *Mother and Child*, 1960–61
Graphite on paper
5 1/2 x 4 1/2 inches (image)
Signed in lower right: Will Barnet

7. Study for *Mother and Child*, c. 1960
Graphite on paper
5 1/2 x 4 1/2 inches (image)
Signed in lower right: Will Barnet
Courtesy Alexandre Gallery, New York

8. Study for *Mother and Child*, c. 1960
Graphite on paper
5 3/4 x 5 inches (image)
Signed in lower right: Will Barnet
Courtesy Alexandre Gallery, New York

9. Study for *Mother and Child*, 1960–61
Ink and graphite on paper
9 3/4 x 9 1/2 inches (sheet)
8 1/2 x 7 1/4 inches (image)
Courtesy Alexandre Gallery, New York

10. Study for *Mother and Child*, c. 1960
Graphite on paper with white heightening
8 1/2 x 7 1/4 inches (image)
Signed in upper right: Will Barnet
This study folded over:
Study for *Mother and Child*, c. 1960
Graphite on paper
8 1/2 x 7 1/4 inches (image)
Signed in upper right: Will Barnet
Courtesy Alexandre Gallery, New York

11. Study for *Mother and Child*, 1960
Graphite on paper
8 1/2 x 7 1/4 inches (image)
Courtesy Alexandre Gallery, New York

12. Study for *Mother and Child*, 1960
Graphite on paper
8 1/2 x 7 1/4 inches (image)
Signed in lower right: Will Barnet
Courtesy Alexandre Gallery, New York

13. Study for *Mother and Child*, c. 1960
Graphite on paper
7 x 4 7/8 inches
Courtesy Alexandre Gallery, New York

14. Study for *Mother and Child*, c. 1960
Graphite on paper
7 x 4 7/8 inches
Courtesy Alexandre Gallery, New York

15. Study for *Mother and Child*, c. 1960
Graphite on paper
7 x 4 7/8 inches
Courtesy Alexandre Gallery, New York

16. Study for *Mother and Child*, c. 1960
Graphite on paper
7 x 4 7/8 inches
Courtesy Alexandre Gallery, New York

17. Study for *Mother and Child*, 1961
Graphite on paper
8 1/4 x 6 1/2 inches
Signed in lower right: Will Barnet '61
Courtesy Alexandre Gallery, New York

18. *Enclosure*, 1962/2003
Oil on canvas
46 x 39 inches
Signed and titled on verso:
Will Barnet 2003/1962 "Enclosure"
Courtesy Alexandre Gallery, New York

19. Studies for *Mother and Child* and *Dark Image*, c. 1960
Graphite on paper
9 1/2 x 18 inches (sheet)
8 1/2 x 7 inches (left image)
5 3/4 x 6 1/2 inches (right image)
Both images signed in lower right: Will Barnet
Collection of the artist
Courtesy Alexandre Gallery, New York

20. Study for *Mother and Child*, 1960
Graphite on paper
11 1/2 x 4 3/4 inches (sheet)
5 1/2 x 4 3/4 inches (image)
Signed in upper right: Will Barnet
Inscribed along lower edge of sheet: Early–abstract study for Mother & Child
Courtesy Alexandre Gallery, New York

21. Studies for *Mother and Child* and *Enclosure*, 1960
Graphite on paper
14 x 9 inches (sheet)
5 1/2 x 4 3/4 inches (both images)
Signed in lower right W.B. (left image) and Will Barnet (right image)
Courtesy Alexandre Gallery, New York

22. Studies for *Enclosure*, c. 1960
Graphite on paper
7 1/2 x 5 inches (sheet)
3 x 2 3/4 inches (both images)
Signed in lower right: WB
Courtesy Alexandre Gallery, New York

23. Study for *Enclosure*, c. 1961
Graphite on paper
9 1/2 x 4 inches (sheet)
5 5/8 x 3 7/8 inches (image)
Signed in lower right: W.B.
Courtesy Alexandre Gallery, New York

24. Study for *Enclosure*, 1961
Gouache and graphite on paper
5 1/2 x 4 5/8 inches (image)
Signed in lower right: Will Barnet
Private collection

25. *Enveloping Forms*, 1963
Color woodcut
27 7/8 x 22 3/4 inches
Courtesy Alexandre Gallery, New York

26. *The Blue Robe*, 1962
Oil on canvas
50 x 54 inches
Signed in lower right: Will Barnet
Collection of the artist
Courtesy Alexandre Gallery, New York

27. Study for *The Blue Robe*, c. 1960
Ink and crayon on paper
8 1/2 x 10 inches
Courtesy Alexandre Gallery, New York

28. Study for *The Blue Robe*, c. 1960
Ink on board
7 3/4 x 9 inches
Signed in lower right: Will Barnet
Courtesy Alexandre Gallery, New York

29. Study for *The Blue Robe*, c. 1960
Ink on board
7 1/16 x 8 7/8 inches
Signed in lower right: Will Barnet
Courtesy Alexandre Gallery, New York

30. Study for *The Blue Robe*, c. 1960
Graphite on paper
9 x 12 inches
Signed in lower right: Will Barnet
Courtesy Alexandre Gallery, New York

31. Study for *The Blue Robe*, c. 1960
Graphite on paper
9 x 12 inches
Signed in lower right: Will Barnet
Courtesy Alexandre Gallery, New York

32. Study for *The Blue Robe*, c. 1960
Graphite on paper
9 x 12 inches
Signed in lower right: Will Barnet
Courtesy Alexandre Gallery, New York

33. Study for *The Blue Robe*, c. 1960
Graphite on paper
12 x 9 inches
Signed in lower right: Will Barnet
Courtesy Alexandre Gallery, New York

34. Study for *The Blue Robe*, c. 1960
Graphite on paper
9 x 12 inches
Courtesy Alexandre Gallery, New York

35. Study for *The Blue Robe*, c. 1960
Graphite on paper
9 x 12 inches
Courtesy Alexandre Gallery, New York

36. Study for *The Blue Robe*, c. 1960
Graphite on paper
9 x 12 inches
Courtesy Alexandre Gallery, New York

37. *The Blue Robe*, 1962
Carbon pencil and conté crayon on paper
21 x 22 1/2 inches (image)
Signed in lower right: Will Barnet 1962
Collection of Mrs. Barbara G. Fleischman

38. *The Robe*, 1964
Aquatint
18 3/4 x 23 7/8 inches (sheet)
12 1/4 x 13 1/4 inches (image)
Titled and signed along lower margin: The Robe artist's proof Will Barnet
Courtesy Alexandre Gallery, New York

39. *Blue Robe*, 1971
Color aquatint
15 11/16 x 21 1/16 inches (sheet)
12 1/4 x 13 1/4 inches (image)
Titled and signed along lower margin: Blue Robe artist's proof Will Barnet
Courtesy Alexandre Gallery, New York

40. *Eden*, 1964–65
Oil on canvas
88 x 43 inches
Signed in lower right: Will Barnet
Courtesy Alexandre Gallery, New York

41. *Black Spokane*, 1964
Oil on canvas
24 1/4 x 10 5/8 inches
Signed and dated on verso: Will Barnet Sept - Dec 1964
Collection of Dr. and Mrs. Lawrence Dubin

42. Study for *Eden*, c. 1964
Watercolor and graphite on paper
10 x 5 inches (sheet)
8 3/8 x 3 3/4 inches (image)
Signed in lower right: Will Barnet
Courtesy Alexandre Gallery, New York

43. Study for Spokane series, c. 1964
Graphite on paper
2 1/4 x 3 1/2 inches (image)
Titled in upper center: Spokane
Signed in lower right: W.B.
Courtesy Alexandre Gallery, New York

44. Study for Spokane series, c. 1964
Graphite and colored pencil on paper
11 3/4 x 8 7/8 inches (sheet)
6 1/4 x 3 7/8 inches (image)
Courtesy Alexandre Gallery, New York

45. Study for Spokane series, c. 1964
Graphite on paper
9 x 12 inches (sheet)
5 1/2 x 10 3/4 inches (image)
Signed in lower right: Will Barnet
Courtesy Alexandre Gallery, New York

46. Study for Spokane series, c. 1964
Graphite on paper
9 x 12 inches (sheet)
6 7/8 x 7 1/4 inches (image)
Signed in lower right: Will Barnet
Courtesy Alexandre Gallery, New York

47. *Eden*, c. 1964
Color etching
26 1/2 x 13 11/16 inches (sheet)
23 3/4 x 10 1/4 inches (image)
Titled in lower left: Eden
Signed in lower right: Will Barnet
Courtesy Alexandre Gallery, New York

48. *Black Spokane*, 1964
Color etching and aquatint
26 x 19 1/8 inches (sheet)
23 5/8 x 10 3/8 inches (image)
Titled and signed along lower margin: Black Spokane trial proof - collage — Will Barnet
Courtesy Alexandre Gallery, New York

49. *Spokane*, c. 1965
Colored etching
28 1/2 x 22 1/4 inches (sheet)
21 3/16 x 13 1/8 inches (image)
Titled in lower left: "Spokane"
Signed in lower right: Will Barnet
Courtesy Alexandre Gallery, New York

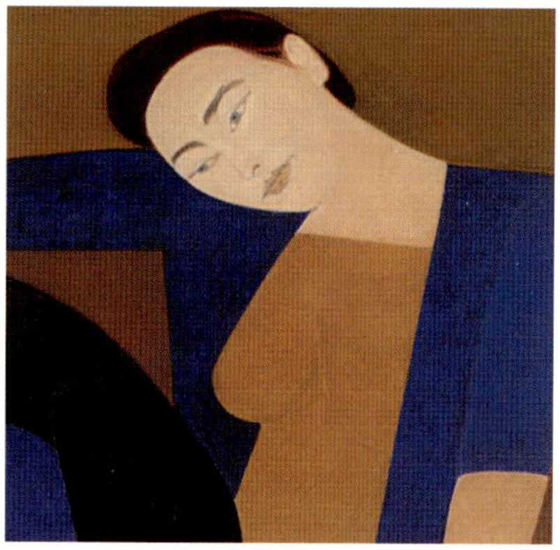

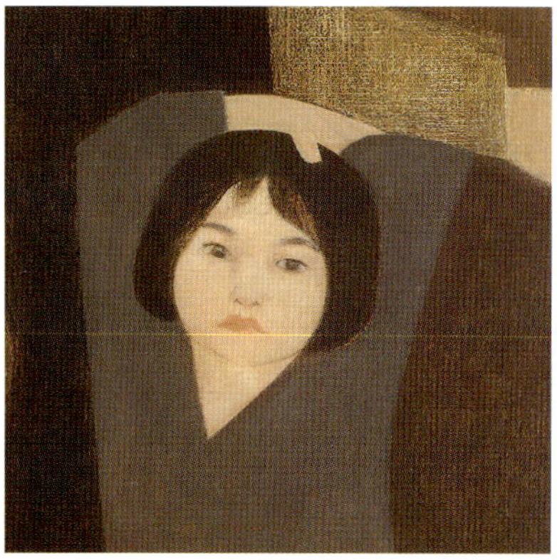

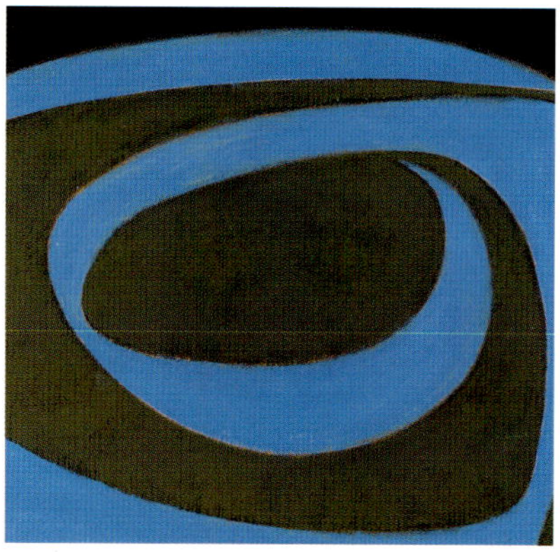